Contents

Introduction

Why another book on booktalking? There are plenty of how-to books out there on this subject but, as we discovered as adult services librarians, we couldn't find a single title that focused entirely on booktalking for adult audiences. Children's and teen services librarians are lucky enough to have scores of books with instruction on and samples of a variety of booktalks for all levels of readers. But where is the poor adult services librarian to go when faced with a library director who's come up with the brilliant idea of going out into the community to promote the library and is now confronted with a roomful of senior citizens anxiously awaiting some sage advice on what to read? Or maybe you have some experience with booktalking to teens, but need some help to change your approach for an adult audience. Or perhaps you've just attended a conference where you saw a booktalk presentation and raved about it to your coworkers—who now expect you to add that to your repertoire. If any of these apply, this book is for you.

We are former youth services librarians who came to adult services with years of experience booktalking to children and teens in both the formal setting of the classroom visit and the informal setting of the library, as well as conducting instructional presentations at county and state library conferences and workshops. As we moved into adult services and were confronted with library patrons and staff who needed assistance with reader's advisory, we discovered the need for booktalking for adults and the lack of material on the subject. We began to offer training to library staff on talking about books with patrons. The goal was to enable them to feel comfortable discussing various genres, authors, and titles with a variety of people. We also began developing adult booktalk presentations for use in the community. At every presentation we were confronted by librarians who told us they wished they could do booktalks but they just didn't know how to start. They wanted to know how to pick the books, how to write the booktalks, and how to present the books in a fresh and entertaining way that would generate interest in the book and bring people to the library. This is why we decided to write this book.

Something to Talk About: Creative Booktalking for Adults is an instruction manual and a material sourcebook in one. The first six chapters provide step-by-step instructions on how to choose a book, write a booktalk, and publicize and present a program for adults. These chapters give information on the benefits of booktalking, explaining what a booktalk is and distinguishing between a booktalk and a book review. They also discuss what makes a book appealing, how to tailor a program for a specific audience, and the different locations at which booktalk programs could be presented to reach out to the community. Chapter 6 gives practical information on what to bring to the program, methods of publicity, checklists, and more.

Chapter 7 offers the reader eighty-eight sample booktalks in eleven different genres: Chillers, General Fiction, Historical Fiction, Humorous Fiction, Multicultural Fiction, Mystery, Nonfiction, Romance, Science Fiction, Sea Adventures, and Women's Fiction. Each booktalk provides bibliographic information on the title as well as a list of genres in which the book could be used. Readers should feel free to use these booktalks as written or to alter them to better fit their own voice.

If you work with adults or are interested in reaching out to adults in your community, this is the book for you. Whether you have never heard of booktalking, whether you are new to the experience or are a seasoned pro, *Something to Talk About: Creative Booktalking for Adults* will provide you with practical information and a wide variety of booktalk samples to enhance your next program. Most of all, we want you to have fun! Although booktalking can be challenging and a little scary, it can also be exciting and rewarding, especially when addressing a roomful of adults ready to be entertained, amused, and informed. Take advantage of the opportunity booktalking offers: You get to go out into the community and talk about your favorite books to readers interested in your opinion and willing to actually read the titles you selected!

We conclude this introduction by listing our top ten myths about booktalking:

TOP TEN MYTHS ABOUT BOOKTALKING

10. Booktalking is extremely difficult and should be done only by professionals.

We're not going to tell you that booktalking is easy and requires no effort. However, most people *can* present booktalks; it just takes three things: practice, practice, and practice!

Practice writing and rewriting your booktalk. When you think it's perfect, practice giving it over and over until it feels comfortable and you can say it without reading it. The next step is practicing the style you are going to use: If you are using props, practice with the props; if you are acting out a scene, practice the scene . . . you get the idea.

Now that you have each booktalk polished, it's time to—you guessed it—practice doing them all together. Arrange the booktalks in different orders until you are comfortable with the flow and pace of the entire presentation. Then practice the entire presentation in front of a mirror, your family, your friends, your pets, and your coworkers. Our rule of thumb is that if our coworkers don't run from the room when they see us coming, we haven't practiced enough.

Why do we go on and on about this? There are two reasons. First, if you are secure in the fact that you know your booktalks, you'll be better able to handle the glitches, questions, and interruptions that *will* occur. Second, in all the universe there are few things that are worse than going to a booktalk presentation and watching someone read a booktalk he or she has taped to the back of the book!

9. I've written or read book reviews before, so a booktalk should be easy; after all, they're the same thing.

A booktalk is not a book review (see chapter 1). A book review passes judgment on a book and then justifies that judgment. For example, "This is an excellent book because it is well written, appropriate for its intended audience, well researched, and accurate." A booktalk assumes that the book is good and acts as a commercial, enticing people to read the book. Consider the differences between a movie review in a newspaper and a television commercial for the same film and you'll see what we mean.

8. Once I learn how to do one type of booktalk, I'm set for life.

There are many methods and styles used to present booktalks, as discussed in chapter 3. Vary the lengths and styles of your booktalks to keep the audience's attention and interest.

7. Nobody/everybody will want to check out the titles I booktalk.

Both of these expectations are unrealistic. Don't set yourself up for failure by expecting everyone in the audience to rush to the library to check out the titles you have booktalked; you will be disappointed. On the other hand, if your booktalks are effective, some people will want to read the books and the demand for these titles will increase. If it's at all possible, don't use a title unless your library carries multiple copies of it. People will become frustrated if they come to the library to check out a book you sold them on and find that the library has only one copy—and it's not available.

6. It doesn't matter whether or not I like a book, I can still use it in my booktalk.

A lot of you are going to disagree with us on this one, but we don't book-talk a title unless we liked it. In a presentation, we consider every book to be a "product" we're trying to sell to the audience. Maybe we're just not good actors, but we think it's very difficult to "sell" a book that we didn't like.

5. Only use new titles in your booktalks. If you use older books everyone will have already read them.

Wrong! There are many "oldies but goodies" out there that people haven't read. Some books with wonderful stories have rotten titles or covers and are passed over for this reason. As we all know, people *do* judge a book by its cover. Other books might be old but are new to your audience. Many quality titles get lost in the crowd or overwhelmed by the latest blockbuster bestseller. For whatever reason a good book might have been missed when it was first published, so booktalking is a great way to draw attention to older titles that may not be circulating anymore.

4. I need to make sure I have an equal number of books for men and women.

This is a little tricky. We do recommend that you select books whose main characters vary in age, gender, race, and so on. Not all titles in a presentation should be about women or Native Americans, for example. Also, you should definitely have a diverse selection of materials that cover various genres, interests, reading levels, and so forth, and include both fiction and nonfiction titles. However, just as you wouldn't label a book as being of interest solely to one race, you shouldn't label a book as being of interest only to a specific gender. Allow audience members to decide for themselves which books interest them.

This myth ties in with myth number three:

3. I can choose books on any subject as long as I have a variety.

Before you decide which titles to use you must know who your audience will be and what is and isn't appropriate for them. This isn't censorship—it's selection! As discussed in chapter 2, the makeup of your audience should impact the titles you select for your booktalk presentation. Remember that you're there to win the audience over, so while a little controversy might be fine, being offensive is not.

2. I don't have to read the book; I can use some of the prepared booktalks available to me in this book. That's why they're there.

While it's certainly true that we hope you find the sample booktalks in chapter 7 useful and good enough to use in some of your presentations, it is *not* our intention that you use them instead of reading the book. In fact, let us say loudly and clearly: READ THE BOOK!

We guarantee that if you give booktalks on titles you haven't read you will eventually get caught. Someday, someone will ask you a question you can't answer or an audience member who has read the book will want to discuss it with you. In any case, you'll have to admit that you haven't read it. You'll be horribly, publicly embarrassed, and you'll lose your credibility. Most audiences will feel betrayed. How can you tell them that a book is worth *their* time and effort to read if it wasn't worth *your* time and effort to read?

Ann-Marie was once in the audience when this happened, and it wasn't a pretty picture. She vowed that it would never happen to her, and there's only one way to make sure: *read the book!*

And the number-one myth about booktalks:

1. A booktalk should give a complete summary of the plot so the audience knows exactly what the book is about.

Raise your right hand and repeat after us: "I promise *never* to tell the ending in a booktalk presentation." Okay, you can put your hand down now.

The purpose of a booktalk is to entice people to read the book. If you give away the ending or a major plot twist, or tell too much of the story, what's the point of audience members reading the book? We know this is difficult and we know that you will have people come up to you after your presentation and beg you to tell them what happens, but *please* stand firm. Allow readers to discover the twists and turns, the laughs and the joys of the story themselves. In the long run they'll thank you for it.

Well, there it is: our list of booktalking myths. We hope it is of some use to you and that you've found some helpful dos and don'ts and some humor. Most of all, we hope you give booktalking a try. It isn't easy; in fact, every time we agree to present a booktalk program, we get nervous. We're worried that no one will like the titles we selected or that we'll bomb. But then we get in front of an audience and they listen (most of them), they ask questions or laugh or gasp (many of them), and they come to the library asking for books we talked about (some of them)—and we realize that it was all worth it and we can't wait to do another booktalk program. The bottom line is, booktalking is very rewarding. Try it, you'll like it!

1

The Benefits of Booktalking

WHAT IS A BOOKTALK?

Put simply, a booktalk is a commercial for a specific book. It can be anywhere from two or three sentences to two or three paragraphs in length. It usually consists of a brief description of the story and characters designed to pique the interest of the audience so they will want to read the book. Most booktalks have a "hook"—something that leaves listeners wanting to know more. This can be an intriguing situation, a tantalizing first line, a mysterious character—anything that will reach out and grab the listener. Think of a booktalk as a movie trailer: Bits and pieces are woven together to capture the audience's interest without giving away the story. A good booktalk is a tease. It might describe a bit of the plot, a quirky character, or an unsettling situation—and just when the listeners are on the edge of their seats, it stops. Now the listeners are involved and want to know more, but the only way they can satisfy their craving is to actually read the book.

It's also important to know what should *not* be included in a booktalk. It is not a book review. By this we mean that a booktalk does not pass judgment on a title. The mere fact that you've chosen that title to talk about means you are recommending the book. (See chapter 3 for more on this.) A booktalk does not include information about the physical layout of the book, for example, font size, binding, illustrations, and so forth. It does not compare a title to the author's previous works or to other books on the same subject or in the same genre. It doesn't justify the literary merit of a title by discussing its writing style, character development, continuity, historical accuracy, and the like. All of these components are important in a book review, but they are disastrous in a booktalk. These details may enlighten and inform, but they do not entertain and intrigue, and they can, in fact, become boring and tedious.

The Booktalk Program

A booktalk program is a presentation involving a series of booktalks, usually on a variety of subjects or genres. It can vary in length from fifteen minutes to an hour. It can stand on its own or be part of a larger presentation, as in a library promotional tour that discusses library services, programs, and collections. It can be done by one person or several people working as a team and can involve skits and/or props to enhance the entertainment value of the program. Booktalk programs are mobile and can be held anywhere, from the comfort of someone's living room to a community center auditorium. In addition, they are easily tailored to accommodate any size audience. Once a catalog of booktalks is developed, they can be used over and over in varying combinations to create different programs that address a variety of needs and interests. See chapter 4 for more information about booktalk programs.

Personal and Professional Benefits of Booktalking

All this sounds like a lot of work, so why do it? Why spend hours and hours reading books, agonizing over the composition of booktalks, the endless practice, and the terrifying aspect of performing in front of strangers—or, worse yet, colleagues? Besides the fact that they're fun to do and personally satisfying—how often do you get applause at work?—booktalking has many professional benefits. First of all, booktalking greatly increases reader's advisory skills by forcing you to read outside your comfort zone. By this we mean reading titles in genres you may not particularly care for or have never tried before. How many times have you either said yourself or heard someone else tell patrons asking for reading suggestions, "I'm sorry. I don't read romance (or mysteries, or adventure, etc.)"? Not only do the patrons leave without getting the help requested, but they may feel judged for their reading preferences.

Effective booktalk programs take into consideration the varying likes and dislikes of the audience. This requires the booktalker to be familiar with titles in all genres. For instance, Kellie doesn't like science fiction and has resisted every effort to get her to read anything in this genre. When Ann-Marie persuaded her to do a booktalking program featuring this genre, an idea was born: "Science Fiction for People Who Don't Like Science Fiction." Kellie managed to find several titles that she enjoyed, and once we created a skit spoofing science fiction conventions, this proved to be one of our more successful presentations. (See chapter 4 for the skit text.) In addition, Kellie now feels more comfortable discussing science fiction when a patron comes to the desk requesting titles in this genre.

The opportunity to develop effective presentation skills is another benefit to booktalking. There's nothing like knowing you're going to be in front of a group of strangers who are counting on you to enlighten and entertain them to force you to practice and improve your public speaking skills. These include enunciation, modulation and volume, eye contact, use of gestures, physical presence, comfort level and audience rapport, and the flow and pacing of the presentation. Effective public speaking skills are always a plus. Once you've mastered the art of booktalking, you can easily parlay the experience to other opportunities in library publicity and promotion, increasing your value in the organization and making you more marketable in the workplace.

Writing is an essential element of the booktalk. Before a talk can be given, it must be written. This is not as easy as it sounds. Something that reads well on paper may not translate well to an oral presentation. Writing a booktalk is a form of speechwriting. Always keep in mind that it's designed to be heard, so attention must be paid to the flow and sound of the words as they are spoken aloud. People aren't going to be able to look up the definition of a word or reread a sentence or paragraph for clarity. Words should be readily understood. Sentences must be short and succinct. Words must be grouped together to roll off the tongue easily so that the speaker doesn't become tongue-tied. The object isn't to amaze the audience with an impressive vocabulary; it's to generate interest in reading a book.

How does writing an effective booktalk help with other aspects of your job? The workplace is all about selling and promotion. You're constantly trying to convince someone to do something, whether you're asking the library director to start a new program, requesting funds from the library board for a new service, or generating citizen support for a new tax bond. The ability to write a persuasive argument will benefit you in all aspects of your career.

Typing at a computer or standing in front of an audience is not the essence of successful booktalking. Talking about books is all about making connections with people. As hard as we might find this to believe, many people find libraries and library staff intimidating. The stereotypical librarian is aloof and stern, and the stereotypical library is a formidable place where books are more important than people. Being able to make one-on-one connections with people, even just one member of a large audience, is vital to reducing their anxiety about visiting and using the library. A successful booktalker becomes the human face of a faceless institution. You are no longer the stranger behind the reference desk; you're the fun person who talked about books at the local community center.

This rapport with patrons can be one of the most rewarding aspects of library work. When people discover that you're willing to talk about books, they not only ask for reading suggestions, they give you reading suggestions. We have learned about some great titles from people stopping at the desk to talk about books they have read, and we have also received insightful feedback on previous recommendations. We've had wonderful conversations about books, authors, and genres that may never have occurred if we hadn't done booktalk programs. Finally, this interaction enables us to keep up to date on the current reading trends and the needs of our community.

The best part of booktalking, in our opinion, is that it's fun. How often, outside the entertainment and sports industries, do people get applauded at work? Where else can you get paid to express your opinions? Where else are you given the freedom of a creative outlet? We have heard booktalks in which presenters use accents and dramatic readings. We have given presentations that utilize props, skits, and songs. This is your opportunity to shine; booktalking gives you the chance to star in your own little show. The only limit to the creativity of your booktalk is your own imagination.

JUSTIFYING A BOOKTALK
PROGRAM TO YOUR BOSS

Developing and performing a booktalk program takes a lot of time and effort. In this era of staff shortages and budget cuts, anything that takes you away from your normal duties will probably need to be justified to the people in charge. The easiest and best way to accomplish this is to explain the benefits of booktalk programs for the library and the community. These include increased visibility and community support, promotion of literacy and reading, and increased library-use statistics.

Booktalk programs will increase library visibility simply because staff members are going out into their community instead of waiting for people to come to them. Booktalking presentations provide the opportunity to promote the materials and services available at the library to an audience that may consist of non–library users. Because of the lighthearted nature of booktalk programs, many in the audience will feel more comfortable asking about other aspects of library use, such as branch locations and hours, how to get a library card, and fees and fines. When people within the community become aware of the personal benefits associated with the library, they are more likely to take ownership of it and support it when needed.

Once library visibility and support are increased, library use will also increase. If people are informed about library materials and services, they will naturally want to use them. Remember, the purpose of a booktalk is to generate interest in reading that book—and that book is available at the library. This means more books will be checked out, which means circulation, attendance, and reference statistics will increase. Many library administrators are interested only in the numbers. Keeping a list of the titles that have been booktalked and showing an increase in circulation of those titles will go a long way toward justifying future presentations.

Does Booktalking Really Increase Circulation?

While anecdotal evidence exists to substantiate the claim that booktalking increases circulation, we found relatively few actual studies to support this with quantitative data. Joni Bodart did one such study as part of a doctoral dissertation in 1984. She conducted a controlled experiment with high school freshmen in which booktalk titles were found to circulate seventeen times more frequently in the year in which they were booktalked than in the previous year, from 15 circulations during the 1983–1984 school year to 266 circulations during the 1984–1985 school year.[1] In another study, conducted in 1993, Eleanor Crowther had similar results. She tracked circulation statistics of middle school students during a twelve-week period and found that circulation increased from 49 to 116 after the booktalking period.[2]

Increased reading and improved literacy is a desired result of any successful booktalk program. According to *Reading at Risk: A Survey of Literary Reading in America*, conducted by the National Endowment for the Arts in 2002, the percentage of adult Americans who read literature has dropped dramatically in the past twenty years. With a 10 percent decline in literary reading, less than half of the adult American population now reads literature. (*Literature* is defined as novels, short stories, plays, or poetry, and *literary reading* is defined as reading such works for pleasure, not for work or school.) The report also found that the percentage of the adult American population reading *any* books has also declined by 7 percent over the past decade.[3] This bleak picture of adult reading makes it clear that something must be done to revitalize adult reading in our communities. Booktalking can be an essential tool in this battle.

In summary, it is easy to see how booktalking will benefit you, your organization, and your community. It will be a lot of work, but it is well worth the time and effort required to create a quality, entertaining program that focuses on reading and literacy. Not only is it fun for the presenter and the audience, the connection that can occur between people who are interested in books is priceless.

NOTES

1. Joni Bodart, "Booktalks Do Work! The Effects of Booktalking on Attitude and Circulation," *Illinois Libraries* 83, no. 6 (June 1986): 378–81.

2. Eleanor Crowther, "Book Talks/Read Alouds, Special Programs, and Service Projects to Encourage Middle School Student Participation in the Library" (PhD diss., Nova University, 1993), ERIC# ED362850.

3. National Endowment for the Arts, *Reading at Risk: A Survey of Literary Reading in America*, Research Division Report #46 (Washington, DC: Author, 2004), p. ix.

2

Choosing the Book

The first challenge of booktalking is finding just the right book. Do you use a best-seller, or a little-known "oldie but goodie"? Should the book be short and sweet, or an epic that consumes the reader? The answer is yes. A book that makes a good booktalk can be any genre, length, or theme. It's difficult to describe the process of finding the right book; sometimes it's a feeling you get after reading something that makes you say to yourself, "This is it." Maybe it's a quirky character that you know will draw smiles from the audience, or it might be a unique setting that takes you to another place and time. Sometimes a book doesn't strike you right away, but you find yourself still thinking about it days later. This is a good indication that the title would make a good booktalk.

First of all, the book must be appealing. What does that mean? According to Joyce Saricks in her book *Reader's Advisory Service in the Public Library*, one way to evaluate a book is to look at what she describes as "appeal characteristics."[1] We'll break these down into four main categories: pacing, characterization, story line, and frame. Let's look at each in more detail.

PACING

Pacing is the flow and momentum of the book. Are the sentences and chapters short, like a suspense novel? Does the book consist mainly of dialogue, or is it filled with lengthy descriptions? Are the characters and plots revealed quickly, or do they unfold slowly? Does the reader have to sort through multiple plotlines, or is there a single, linear plot? What about the characters? Do they drive the plot or react to it? And finally, does the book come to a final conclusion, or does it leave the reader with unanswered questions? All of this contributes to the pacing of the book, which has very little to do with the number of pages it contains. A long book such as *The Time Traveler's Wife* by Audrey Niffenegger, which is more than five hundred pages long, is a "quick read" because it tells the story in little snippets that move through different time periods and build to a dramatic conclusion that is foreshadowed throughout the story. On the other hand, *The Education of Arnold Hitler* by Marc Estrin, while interesting, goes into great detail about every aspect of the main character's life. This drastically slows the action down and causes the book to be less compelling and engaging. It's a good book, but a slow read.

CHARACTERIZATION

Characterization is all about the characters in the novel. Who tells the story? Is it a first-person narrative, is it told from the perspective of another person in the story, or is it told by the voice of an objective narrator? The point of view is one of the most important elements of the novel because it affects the tone of the story and the expectations of the reader. For instance, if the story is told through the eyes of a child, as in *To Kill a Mockingbird*, the reader doesn't expect an in-depth analysis of racial relations in society of the 1930s, which they might expect if the story were told by the adult Atticus.

When examining the aspects of characterization, it is important to note that there are other factors to consider. Is the focus on a single character or several characters whose lives are intertwined? Are the characters developed over time, or are they stereotypes we recognize immediately? Is the reader expected to observe the characters impersonally or relate to them? Are the secondary characters memorable and important to the plot, or is their function just to fill in the story and provide background? Are the characters realistic and their motivations and actions believable? By this we mean that effectively developed characters are consistent and reliable. They touch us and make us care about them even if they are supposed to be bad. Characters are the reader's buy-in to the book. They are the reason for the story and often the reason we pick up the book in the first place. Their lives, experiences, relationships, and adventures provide an avenue for the reader to acquire new insights or escape from their own lives. The appeal of characters has nothing to do with whether they are good or evil, but rather with whether they are engaging and three-dimensional.

STORY LINE

The story line is the plot of the novel and deals with the author's intention for the book. Does the story emphasize people, situations, or events? Is the focus of the story more introspective and psychological or external and action oriented? Another way of describing this is that the story can be character driven or plot driven.

A story that is character driven is focused on the characters. It's not the events that happen that move the story along, it's how the characters react to those events and to other characters that make the story. For example, *These Is My Words* by Nancy Turner is the story of Sarah Prine, a young girl growing up in Arizona Territory. While we learn many historical details about life on the frontier, it is not the focus of the book. The focus is Sarah's life and how she grows from a barely literate teenager to the self-possessed matriarch of a pioneer family. An example of a plot-driven book is *The Rich Part of Life* by Jim Kokoris, in which a widower with two boys wins the lottery. While the characters are appealing in their quirkiness, the story is moved along by a single event and its aftermath.

FRAME

When we talk about the frame of a book, we are describing several things: tone, atmosphere, setting, and background. Although they may be subtle, they are vital to the reading experience. Often we are in a mood to read a book with a certain tone, or setting, and this affects what we select.

Tone

Tone is the emotional map of the novel. It is the tool used by the author to take the reader on a personal journey of mental state or disposition. The tone can range from dark and foreboding to lighthearted and humorous. It evokes a feeling in the reader based on word choice, setting, use of dialogue, descriptions, and other details. *Rebecca* by Daphne du Maurier is an example of a dark and foreboding tone. By letting readers know of the main character's insecurities and fears, coupled with the sinister superiority of the housekeeper, the aloofness of the husband, and a big old scary house, the author foreshadows the bad things that are going to happen. In contrast, *The Boy Next Door*, by Meg Cabot, takes place in a contemporary setting, and although it contains a murder, the lighthearted dialogue and unique e-mail format give it a whimsical and humorous tone.

Atmosphere

Atmosphere describes the intangible parts of the characters' surroundings. The main difference between atmosphere and tone is that the tone is consistent throughout the story, whereas the atmosphere is situational and can—

and usually does—change. Atmosphere can involve weather, lighting, time, place—even the emotionally charged feeling in a room when characters have just had an argument. Rain is used often in *Rebecca* to evoke a feeling of impending doom in the main character, Mrs. de Winter—and the reader: It is raining when she first meets the sinister housekeeper, it is raining when she discovers a tragic secret about Rebecca, and it is raining the night of her humiliation at the costume ball.

Setting

Setting is the physical place or places in which the novel is set. Its importance is that it gives the reader a frame of reference for the plot and the characters. The setting can provide motivation for action, background information on the characters, and details to flesh out the story and make it believable. Setting can be vital to set the mood of the story, or it can be a generic neighborhood anywhere, which doesn't factor much into the novel. For example, an isolated mansion in the English countryside of a bygone era is an important element in *Rebecca*; it would not be the same story if it were set in a large city in contemporary times. Ghost stories lend themselves to this setting. On the other hand, *The Boy Next Door* could be set in any large metropolis. The character could live in an apartment or a house and work in any major corporation.

Background

Background deals with information about the characters, setting, or plot that occur either before the story began or outside the story's main focus—in other words, "off-camera." There are several ways to provide the reader with this missing information. Sometimes it is given in flashbacks, dreams, or dialogue with other characters. Sometimes the narrator provides the background needed to understand a particular event in the story. It can be delivered all at once, or revealed slowly throughout the course of the novel. Other times, the background information is never revealed at all. For example, in *Rebecca*, the second Mrs. de Winter, although a major character, is never given a name. By withholding this information, the author makes a statement about the character's feelings of insignificance and unimportance in relation to the other characters.

So why are pacing, characterization, story line, and frame important? Without even realizing it, we are constantly using appeal characteristics to judge the quality of a book. Remember, the purpose of a booktalk is to generate interest in a particular title—to persuade someone that a book is worth reading. To do that, we must find the hook that will appeal to readers. As described in chapter 1, the hook is what grabs the audience's attention and motivates them to read the book. Although the characteristic terminology (pacing, characterization, story line, and frame) would never be used in an actual booktalk, we include them here to help you learn how to select an appropriate title.

WHAT KINDS OF BOOKS MAKE GOOD BOOKTALKS?

There is no single type of book that makes a good booktalk. Every person is different and has different strengths and weaknesses when it comes to creating a booktalk. That said, there are some common elements to consider.

First, you must read the book. As silly as this sounds, it is important. While there are many preprepared booktalks available (look in chapter 7 of this book, for instance) they should be used only after—and not instead of—reading the book. After a booktalk, audience members often ask questions about a title, or someone who has read the book may want to discuss it with you. If you haven't read the book yourself, you will be found out and not only suffer embarrassment but also lose your credibility. People will question why they should take the time to read something when you didn't bother to read it yourself. They may also begin to wonder if you actually read any of the titles you just booktalked. In addition, you have to read the book to determine whether you like it or not. This is essential in giving the booktalk your own voice and lending it sincerity and authenticity.

Second, you have to like the book. There are those in the profession who would argue this point, but we feel very strongly that liking the book yourself is important in convincing others that they would like it. This doesn't mean you have to absolutely love the title, or think it was the best thing you ever read. It doesn't have to be particularly well written or even have any literary merit whatsoever, but it does need to be appealing in some way. The mere fact that the title has been selected for a booktalk demonstrates to the audience that you feel it is worthy of their time: that you liked it and think they will enjoy reading it as well.

Third, you need to be able to find a hook—that one aspect of the story that will serve as the central theme of your booktalk. This will vary not only from person to person but also from title to title. For example, if you are good at doing accents, a quirky southern character might provide the perfect opportunity to showcase your talent by taking on the persona of the character in the booktalk. Another book might contain a situation or event that lends itself to becoming the hook. Settings—a tropical locale, for instance—provide another means of attracting the audience to your title. Effective booktalks depend on the presenter's ability to identify and articulate that quality that makes a particular title unique and interesting to a potential audience.

Perhaps one of the best ways to explain the procedure of book selection is to list the characteristics that tend to make a title *undesirable* to use for a booktalk.

1. The book is too complex to be adequately described in a one- to two-minute booktalk. This might mean there are too many characters or plotlines, or that there is no one element that stands out from the rest.
2. The book does not have wide appeal. The subject matter might be too controversial, the book might contain an excessive amount of sex or violence, or the language might be offensive in some way.
3. The book is too limited in content. Perhaps the plot is formulaic, or the characters are weak, or the story line does not have enough depth to make it unique. For instance, while you may enjoy reading a Harlequin romance, it wouldn't provide enough substance to booktalk.
4. The book is too dry or pedantic. Sometimes an author gets bogged down in theories, details, and the desire to educate readers. While this may work well in a nonfiction book, it can detract from a novel's readability.
5. The book is too preachy or has an agenda. Some books are written to persuade rather than entertain. Such titles don't lend themselves to booktalking for a public audience because as a representative of a public institution, you may not want to appear to advocate a particular viewpoint.
6. The book is not appropriate for a current political climate. An example of this is that after 9/11, titles with themes that focused on Middle Eastern cultures, religion, or acts of terrorism would not be received in the same spirit as they would have been before 9/11.
7. The book is not appropriate for a particular audience. Examples of this include booktalking romance books to a group of male executives, promoting teen books at a senior center, and highlighting war stories to a group of pacifists.
8. The book is a blockbuster best-seller. Remember that the purpose of a booktalk is to promote lesser-known titles and to increase circulation. Blockbusters don't need this kind of promotion; most people are already aware of them. In addition, blockbusters usually have long waiting lists, and this will prove frustrating to audience members who visit the library to check out a particular title only to find it unavailable.

PRACTICAL CONSIDERATIONS IN BOOK SELECTION

We have found a few things to be helpful when choosing a book for a booktalk:

- Use a mix of older and newer titles. When you are searching for a good book to use in a booktalk, older titles that are sitting on the shelves, unused because no one knows about them, may provide the perfect balance in a booktalk presentation, especially when built around a theme. Many times quality titles get overshadowed by best-sellers, and although you know people would enjoy reading them, they get lost in the shuffle and go unread. Booktalking will give these titles new life.
- Use nonfiction to provide balance. Many readers prefer nonfiction to novels, and using a few nonfiction titles in your presentation will make it more inclusive and appealing to all audience members. There are many nonfiction titles that read like fiction, which, when booktalked, could persuade strict fiction readers to try a nonfiction title and broaden their reading repertoire. One way to accomplish this is to pair a nonfiction title and a fiction title on the same subject. An example of this is the novel *Grand Ambition* by Barbara Michaels and the nonfiction *Sunk without a Sound* by Brad Dimock, which both deal with the disappearance of a young honeymooning couple as they travel down the Colorado River in the Grand Canyon. (Booktalks for these titles are available in chapter 7.)
- People *do* judge a book by its cover. Never use a re-bound copy in your program, because it doesn't offer the audience anything to see. If a book has a great cover, the job of selling it is a bit easier, but don't reject a title just because the cover is unappealing. In fact, the contrast between the bad cover and the really good story inside could be the hook you use to make it more appealing to others.
- Make sure your library has multiple copies of the title you're recommending. Avoid patron frustration by making sure the books will be available to patrons when they visit the library.

NOTE

1. Joyce G. Saricks and Nancy Brown, *Reader's Advisory Service in the Public Library* (Chicago: American Library Association, 1997), p. 35.

3

How to Write a Booktalk

WHAT'S THE HOOK?

As described in chapter 2, it is difficult to define what exactly a hook is. We think the simplest definition of a hook is that it's the essence of the story—an intangible "something" that compels you to keep reading a particular book or that "something" that stays with you long after you've read it. It's the first thing that comes to mind when you describe the book to someone else. It could be a unique situation, a setting, a feeling that's invoked by the story line, a quirky character—anything that speaks to the reader and makes the book an enjoyable reading experience. Sometimes the hook doesn't appear right away; it may take a day or two of reflection before it becomes apparent. The hook is what completes this sentence: "I just read the most amazing book. It's . . ."

TYPES OF BOOKTALKS

Finding the hook is essential because it helps to determine what kind of booktalk you're going to write. There are as many different types of booktalks as there are booktalkers. We've come up with nine general categories. Let's look at each of them in detail.

Prop Booktalk

Sometimes a story or a character lends itself to the use of one or more props. This can range from something as simple as wearing a hat to something as complex as juggling. We once did a whole presentation about sea adventures sitting in a big yellow rubber raft, pretending to be lost at sea. In

15

some instances, a character is associated with a particular object, such as Sherlock Holmes with his pipe or Mary Poppins with her umbrella. Many props are easily available and can visually enhance a booktalk by creating an instant interest before you even begin talking. The use of props can also interject humor or drama into an otherwise dry presentation. Props should be used sparingly, not with every booktalk in a presentation, or they become a distraction, which lessens their effect. Make sure the prop is big enough to be seen by the audience. The number-one rule with using props is to practice! You must be comfortable with how they are incorporated into your presentation, or it could be disastrous; for example, if you're going to juggle, make sure you actually know how to juggle. The purpose of using props is to attract the attention of the audience and entertain them in a positive way, not to distract them from your talk or make you look like a fool.

Skits

Skits are a wonderful way to maintain the flow of a presentation that is conducted by two or more people. It puts the series of booktalks in a larger context. For example, when we did a presentation on science fiction titles for people who don't like science fiction, we created a skit in which we were addressing a science fiction convention and the audience played the part of convention attendees (see chapter 4). We began the program by leading the audience in a pledge and ended with a song. Our presentation was intended to be humorous—we wore silly hats and buttons and parodied fanatic science fiction aficionados. The success of the presentation was demonstrated by the rapt attention of the audience. Skits are not only entertaining, they provide an alternative to a lecture format and encourage audience participation. The key to successfully using a skit in your presentation is to be totally committed to it. If you are uncomfortable performing the skit, the audience will be uncomfortable watching it and your program will fail.

Accents

Many novels are set in a particular place, which may lend itself to the use of accents. This is especially true if the story takes place in the South or in a foreign country, and if the booktalk takes on the persona of a particular character in the book. The use of accents can bring the characters to life and provide the perfect hook for your booktalk. However, only a booktalker skilled in accents can pull this off. Again, you want to enhance your booktalk, not distract from it. Nothing makes an audience cringe like a bad accent.

Being in Character

There are many ways to be in character. We've already discussed how props and accents can be used to illustrate a character, but there are other ways to bring a character to life. Perhaps the character has a distinctive walk, gesture, or way of standing. Maybe there's nothing distinctive about the character, but you take on his or her persona and address the audience as if you were that character. Using diary entries and letters is an additional method of portraying the story through the eyes of a character. The key to this type of booktalk is to be consistent. If you decide to do the booktalk from a character's point of view, then you must stay in character throughout, otherwise it could be confusing to the audience.

Dramatic Reading

Although they should be used very sparingly—because it can become tedious to listen to someone reading straight from the book—dramatic readings can be an effective hook to a particular kind of book. A dramatic reading is when you literally read an excerpt, verbatim, from the book. This can be particularly successful with poetry, diaries, books written in a specific dialect, and nontraditional stories. It can also be used for a specific passage that perfectly encapsulates the story or character. This passage can be humorous, suspenseful, or the ultimate cliffhanger. The key to this kind of booktalk is to keep it short. The last thing people want to see is someone standing in front of them reading multiple pages from a book.

Cliffhangers

Cliffhangers are especially effective as booktalks. A cliffhanger is when you set up a situation or a scene in which tension builds, only to leave the audience hanging at the conclusion. The only way they can satisfy their curiosity is to actually read the book. Books that lend themselves to the cliffhanger booktalk include mysteries, thrillers, crisis fiction, adventure, survival, espionage, and psychological suspense, but any story that has a dramatic climax might lend itself to this type of booktalk.

Reporter

The reporting booktalk is characterized by an objective account of a specific event from the book. This is often written as if it will appear in a newspaper or on a television news program. It is designed to be passive and impersonal in order to convey specific information or details about an event without becoming emotionally involved. This is particularly effective when used to highlight an overwhelming situation contained within the story. The contrast between the objective retelling and the emotionally charged event enhances the impact of the booktalk. Nonfiction books, especially true crime, often lend themselves to this format. Fiction books that portray shocking events also work well with this type of booktalk.

Humorous

People love to laugh. The humorous booktalk is often the perfect way to capture the audience's attention and interest. There are many ways to write a humorous booktalk, whether it's using a catchy phrase or emphasizing a silly situation, or even using a prop, a look, or a gesture. Humor is often conveyed through the presentation rather than in the words on the paper. It's the way you say the words, not the words themselves, that provide the laugh. While lighthearted books lend themselves most readily to this type of booktalk, don't be afraid to interject some humor when doing booktalks for other genres.

Audience Participation

Audience participation occurs whenever the audience is directly involved in a booktalk. This can be accomplished by asking questions, recruiting volunteers, having the audience repeat a phrase, enlisting their help to sing, and so on. This can be one of the most entertaining and fun ways to liven up a presentation and heighten audience interest.

Synopsis

The synopsis consists of a *brief* summary of the story, still using the hook to generate interest in the title. Although this is the most common type of booktalk, it's also the most problematic. Many inexperienced booktalkers tell too much of the story. The summary should not reveal every plotline, character, and dilemma and must *never* give away the ending. If you give too much away, there's no point in reading the story and the booktalk becomes too long, boring, and pointless. You should always leave the audience wanting more, with unanswered questions, in order to motivate them to read the book.

Variety is the spice of life, and booktalks are no exception. Utilize more than one type of booktalk in your presentations to keep the audience alert and involved. Experiment with various booktalk formats, practicing in front of mirrors, family, friends, and colleagues until it feels right. Not only will your audience appreciate it, you will feel more energized and engaged when you vary the styles of your booktalks.

WRITING STYLE

Everyone has a different writing style, but every effective booktalk has to incorporate the same specific elements. These include:

- Easily understood vocabulary. You are not trying to impress them with big words; you are trying to motivate them to read a book. Your audience is not going to have a dictionary handy and if they can't understand what you are saying, they will tune you out.
- Short and succinct sentences. Not only does this make the booktalk easier to follow, but it makes it easier to remember and present. Unlike the printed word, a speech does not allow the audience to reread a section for clarity.
- Easy flow. Pay attention to the words you select and how they sound together. Certain words when used together will enhance the flow of the presentation. Others don't flow together; the speaker has to stop abruptly after one word to try to form the next. This not only leads to a choppy delivery but also can turn your booktalk into a tongue twister. On the other hand, alliteration, in which the same sound is repeated, is appealing to the ear as long as it's not overused. Practicing the booktalk aloud as it is being written will assist you in selecting the right words, as well as perfecting it after the writing is completed.
- Brevity. Booktalks should not be more than one or two minutes in length. Occasionally a booktalk may require more time, as when using audience participation or a skit, but this is rare. In most cases, anything longer than two minutes will cause the audience to lose focus.

STEPS IN WRITING A BOOKTALK

1. Once you've selected a title to booktalk, jot down pertinent facts and names from the story that you want to incorporate into the booktalk. This should include characters' names, places, key events, plot sequences—anything you want to remember when creating your booktalk.

    Start writing. Don't get bogged down in word selection or sentence structure at this time. What is the hook that made you select this title to booktalk? What element of the book was important to you as a reader? Use the hook and write the booktalk around that, incorporating your key elements. Don't worry about length, pacing, or flow here. Your goal in this step is to capture the feelings the story invoked.

2. First impressions are important. Constructing an effective opening sentence is your first hurdle in writing a quality booktalk. It has to capture the listener's attention immediately. Don't feel that a booktalk always has to begin with the beginning of the book. It is sometimes more effective to begin in the middle of the story, or tease the audience with a suspenseful event or a character's dilemma. Don't use phrases like "I

liked this book because . . ." or "This book is about . . ." Choose dynamic, attention-grabbing words and phrases.

3. Likewise, the ending of your booktalk is vitally important. It is the last impression your audience will have and should leave them in a heightened emotional state. Construct your final sentence with the goal of lasting impact. This can be accomplished through either a long sentence that builds suspense or a short sentence that finishes a thought in a way the audience will remember.

4. Once you've completed the first draft, read it over. Does it include the highlights of the story? Is the information accurate and in the right sequence? Is there enough of it to represent the plot in an understandable way? The goal is to provide enough of the story to pique interest but not so much that it ruins the reading experience. If the first draft doesn't accomplish this, continue to rewrite and revise until it has the impact you're looking for.

5. Once you've revised and reworked the booktalk, read it aloud to yourself. This is the time to correct sentence structure, pacing, word selection, and flow. How does the booktalk sound? Is it difficult to say? If it's difficult to say smoothly now, when you're alone, relaxed, and reading it from the page, how hard will it be to present when you're nervous, standing in front of an audience? Your goal is simplicity with impact.

6. Set the booktalk aside for a while. Sometimes you get so close to the writing, so bogged down in the mechanics of the booktalk, that you need to take a break from it. This enables you to look at it later with fresh eyes in order to make sure the effect is what you want. Things to watch out for include repetitive use of the same words, too many adjectives, or a lack of strong and vivid words. Consulting a thesaurus may prove useful at this time. Also look at the overall content to determine if you've given away too much of the story. Have you included too many plotlines, characters, events, or other details?

7. Now that your booktalk reads smoothly and you're happy with the flow, time yourself. Length does matter. As stated earlier, booktalks should generally be one to two minutes in length. At this point in the writing process, most booktalks are too long. If this is true for you, you will need to start taking out things in your booktalk that are not essential to the story, such as secondary plotlines and nonessential events. You may also decide to revise your word choice in order to maximize the impact and minimize the number of words used. By this we mean that you should use words that impart a lot of description, imagery, and punch so that you can use fewer words overall.

8. Now your booktalk is perfect, right? Wrong. It still has to pass the colleague test. Choose someone whose opinion you value and read it

Here are some tips for creating outstanding speeches, according to Philip R. Theibert in *How to Give a Damn Good Speech*.[1]

- Use fragments for impact
- Use alliteration
- Repeat a word or phrase at the start or end of your speech
- Create a rhyming effect with short phrases
- Use a poem or limerick
- Use an amazing fact
- Use short words to make a point
- Alternate short and more complex sentences
- Vary verbs
- Change tone to get the attention of the audience
- Use dialogue
- Use current events
- Start with something shocking
- Use statistics

aloud to him or her. Ask for an honest reaction to the booktalk. If possible, ask two different people for feedback—one person who has read the book and one person who has not read the book. This is beneficial because the person who has read the book can verify that you've captured the important events of the story. The person who hasn't read the book can tell you if the booktalk made sense and succeeded in creating an interest in reading the book. Watch their reactions as you give the booktalk. Do their eyes glaze over in spots? Do they laugh at the right times? Are they appropriately shocked, dismayed, or saddened? Does the talk get bogged down or lag anywhere? Your colleagues can advise you on areas that need to be tightened up, explained further, or eliminated. This step is essential because reading your booktalk aloud to someone else is a first rehearsal for presenting it to an audience. It is also a good test of your comfort level with the specific booktalk. Don't expect too much comfort at this time, however; that will come later, with practice.

9. Don't be discouraged. Writing a booktalk is not an easy thing to do, especially when you are just starting out. Hearing criticism is never pleasant, but you've chosen these colleagues for a test run because you value and respect their opinions. It's much better to hear about the booktalk's faults now, when you are able to fix them, than to have that

booktalk fall flat in front of an audience. We have written hundreds of booktalks and never has one been perfect from the very beginning. It takes rethinking, rewriting, and revising to create a booktalk with punch and pizzazz.

Writing the booktalk is the hardest and most important aspect of the booktalking experience. Don't rush it and don't be discouraged. If it doesn't feel right, it can throw your whole presentation off, so take all the time you need to make it perfect. There are no shortcuts to creating a great booktalk. It takes patience, time, and practice. While we wish we could assure you that creating booktalks gets easier with time and experience, it doesn't. We still agonize over every booktalk we create—and we still follow all the steps listed above. What *does* come with practice and experience is confidence in two essential areas: first, that you *are* capable of writing an effective booktalk; and second, that you have the ability to *recognize* a quality booktalk when you've created one.

NOTE

1. Philip R. Theibert, *How to Give a Damn Good Speech* (New York: Galahad, 2000), 49–79.

4

Putting a Program Together

Now that you have a number of booktalks written and prepared, it's time to put a program together. Although some may think a program is just several booktalks strung together, it is not that simple. There are seven elements to consider when preparing a booktalk program: audience, themes, locales, solo versus partners, props and skits, booktalk order, and presentation skills.

AUDIENCE

Knowing in advance the makeup of your audience is important. Not only will it help decide which titles to talk about, it will affect every other aspect of the program. You want to develop a program that will entertain and inform, not offend and disappoint. Some things to consider, if possible, are the age, gender, race, religion, education, and profession of the audience. These demographics will influence your choices, as different titles will appeal to specific kinds of audiences. For instance, the Kiwanis Club is probably not going to be interested in a program featuring booktalks on epic romances. Nor will the local church women's group be thrilled with a program of titles that focus on graphic sex or violence. This is why it is important to develop a whole repertoire of booktalks. The more booktalks you have written and ready to go, the easier it will be to pick and choose titles that are appropriate for a particular audience. This does not mean that you should fall into the trap of stereotyping your audience. Don't assume that a group of senior citizens is interested only in gentle reads or classics. It's a good idea to check with the coordinator to see if there are any restrictions, or to learn whether the group has special interests or preferences that will help you choose appropriate and interesting titles.

The makeup of the audience will also affect other aspects of the program.

Some groups will be more receptive than others to the use of props. Some audiences will appreciate a skit; others will find it inappropriate or frustrating. In addition, the type of skit or prop you use will be affected by the makeup of the audience. A skit that is highly successful with one group could be considered silly, distracting, offensive, or even insulting by another group. Our science fiction convention parody is a good example of this. While a group of librarians found it highly entertaining, we would never have presented it to a science fiction club for fear of insulting them. (See figure 4.1 for the complete script.)

There are definite advantages to being a segment of a larger program, from both the perspective of the presenter and the perspective of the audience. For one thing, you don't have to prepare as much material. Your total time commitment will be much less since you have fewer booktalks to practice and remember. Also, the success of the program does not rest squarely on your shoulders, so there's less pressure and anxiety. And because a large program provides a variety of presenters, the audience is more attentive to each speaker and less likely to get bored. The disadvantages to being part of a large program include coordination with other presenters, working within a strict time limit, placement within the program (right after lunch, at the end of the day, etc.), and coinciding with the overall purpose of the program.

The reason the group is gathered is an important consideration for the booktalker. Are they having a meeting in which you are a small part, or are they coming just to hear your presentation? Are they avid readers who are looking for new ideas, or are they non–library users who have to be persuaded to pick up a book? If the group has an agenda, in which you are but a part, try to find out how you fit into the overall program and their expectations. You might discover that they don't want a booktalk presentation at all; instead, they want information about library services and resources specific to their group. If this is the case, your entertaining booktalk presentation will fall flat.

Speaking of falling flat, be careful of audience participation. Using the audience as part of your presentation is highly effective if they are gathered to be entertained and if you've previously established a relationship with some of the members. It has been our experience that several factors contribute to the success of audience participation. First, they have to be at the program willingly—not coerced or required to attend. Second, they have to be interested in hearing about books and have come to the program expressly for that purpose. And third, there has to be an element of trust between you and the audience. Since audience participation is dependent upon members feeling comfortable enough to participate knowing you won't make them look ridiculous, you have to have previously established a relationship with them. This could be achieved through previous programs or meeting some members prior to the program.

Figure 4.1. Sample Skit

Read Sci-Fi and Prosper!

Ann-Marie: All right, all right. Let us have your attention please; play time is over! We have a lot to do today and not much time.

Kellie: I hereby open this fifth annual conference of the **W**orldwide **E**xtraterrestrial **I**nvestigators **R**eading **D**aily **O**n **E**verything **S**ci-Fi. Please stand for the official WEIRDOES pledge.

Ann-Marie and Kellie: Science fiction is our life
Reading it does not cause strife
When at work and when at play
We read sci-fi every day!

Kellie: Thank you; you may be seated. Now, down to business, first on our agenda is recruiting new members. I'm very distressed to report that we are way behind in our quota of three new sci-fi readers per year. Now it's true that my husband, Spock, did recruit his cousin Betty . . .

Ann-Marie: . . . now named Uhura—

Kellie: . . . yes, and she did come to one meeting, but she was discovered reading Harlequin romances during small group exercises.

Ann-Marie: I just don't understand how this could happen. All of you know how important it is to get people to read science fiction . . .

Kellie: . . . and, you know how much we pout when our goal isn't met;

Ann-Marie: . . . and everyone knows how many potential WEIRDOES live in Arizona. So the only thing we can figure is that you're not promoting the right science fiction books.

Kellie: With this in mind, at our last executive board meeting we determined titles that will assist you in converting new readers to this galactic genre.

Ann-Marie: You'll find these listed in your WEIRDOES manual. For those of you who didn't bring your manual today, please refer to the Run for Your Life . . . It's Science Fiction list, available on the table in the back of the room.

Kellie: In addition, we've developed some tricks—er, I mean tips, to help you lure unsuspecting book browsers into our midst.

Ann-Marie: First, don't use the term "science fiction"; it scares kosmickies . . .

Kellie: . . . you know, those people afraid of sci-fi.

Ann-Marie: Use friendly words like "heavenly," "adventuresome," or "far out" to describe these books.

Kellie: Far out? You'd actually say FAR OUT? Next you'll be telling them the book is really groovy, man! Anyway, also, remember that a lot of sci-fi has characteristics that resemble other genres like romance, mystery, or historical fiction.

Ann-Marie: Yeah, you can reel them in with tantalizing historical tidbits and once they're hooked, they won't even notice the sci-fi. Take *Doomsday Book* by Connie Willis, for example . . .

Figure 4.1.   (Continued)

(Begin booktalk of *Doomsday Book* by Connie Willis, continue with
booktalks, alternating between presenters)

(At END of program)

Ann-Marie: See, it's fun to read sci-fi and easy to talk about this wonderful
genre. So go out and recruit, recruit, recruit and next year, we'll be over our
quota! Just remember:

Ann-Marie and Kellie: (singing to the tune of "Twinkle, Twinkle, Little Star")

> Science fiction is okay,
> Don't let it scare you away.
> Time travel can be such fun,
> Aliens have you on the run.
> Steamy sex and future crooks,
> You'll find it all in sci-fi books.
>
> Read Sci-Fi and Prosper!

THEMES

Sometimes it is appropriate to create a theme-based presentation. If the
group has a specific interest, like a mystery reading group, this theme would
reflect their particular needs. One of the benefits of providing a theme-based
program is that you know the audience is already interested in the subject.
Another benefit to using themes is that they lend themselves more readily to
skits, and they have the potential to be more entertaining to the audience as
well as the presenter. A theme-based presentation is especially helpful when
your booktalks are part of a larger presentation, such as a workshop in
which each presenter might select a different theme in order to vary the program. Finding titles that fit a particular theme can be challenging and
rewarding, and theme-based programs are often the most requested.

Themes can allow you to return to the same venue repeatedly, reaching a
different group of people with each visit. An example of this is programs at
a retirement community. It is possible to schedule a booktalk each month
and vary the programs by theme. One month a presentation on mysteries;
the next, romance; the next, science fiction, and so on. In this way, you can
return to the same venue over and over, reaching a new audience with each
visit. However, there is a danger in doing a theme-based program. Often,
people who are not interested in a particular theme or genre will not attend
your program, and so you have lost the opportunity to promote the library

---

Skip a Skit: When a Skit Is Not a Good Idea

- The audience lacks the proper language skills to understand. For example, an ESL class with new learners who won't get the jokes.
- The audience relies upon an interpreter or translator. For example, a group of the hearing impaired.
- The audience is focused on factual information and would consider a skit to be silly and extraneous. For example, a group of business owners who have come to a program on using the library.
- The audience is large and there is no sound system. A booktalk can be projected; a skit cannot.

---

and its collections to them. Another disadvantage to using themes is that the audience may already be expert readers in the subject and have unreasonably high expectations. Failure to meet these expectations could result in a loss of credibility and failure to positively represent the library. It's more common and often easier to do a general booktalk program in which a mix of genres and subjects are selected. This enables the booktalker to meet the needs of a variety of reading interests with one program and connect to a larger number of people in a positive way.

VENUES

Where is the presentation going to be held? The easiest place, of course, is in your own library because you are familiar with and have control over your own facility. However, the library is seldom the venue of choice for outside organizations. Since one of the justifications and benefits of booktalking is to reach out to the community, travel to outside venues is often required. It is vital to visit the venues in advance of the presentation in order to familiarize yourself with the physical aspects that may affect your performance. Knowing the limitations of the location will enable you to plan accordingly and eliminate the stress of uncertainty. There's nothing worse than arriving at the site and discovering that there's no sound system and that two hundred people are expected. Some physical limitations can't be changed, but knowing about them will enable you to work within their strictures. Others can be fixed before the program begins. In the example above, a booktalker may be able to bring a portable sound system if he or she knows in advance that one is needed. The following is a brief description of possible problems and solutions regarding booktalking venues.

Room Temperature

Remember that rooms are warmer when they are filled with people. How's the temperature when no one is there? If you are expecting a large crowd, it is a good idea to lower the temperature a couple of hours beforehand. A small group in a large room may need to have the temperature raised before they arrive to maximize their comfort (and yours). Arrange this with the event coordinator well in advance of the program.

Visual Obstructions

Make sure that the room is cleared of unnecessary items that can limit the audience's view of the performing area. If pillars or posts are an obstruction, rearrange chairs to minimize the problem. Walk around the room to determine where you should stand in order to provide the best visibility to the audience.

Lighting

Is there any flexibility to the lighting situation in the room? Usually it's best to have the room bright and well lit. This enables the audience to see facial expressions, props, booklists, and so on. If the lighting is not adequate, consider turning this potential problem into an asset, for example, to add atmosphere to a more dramatic booktalk presentation.

Sound

Sound can include the acoustics of the room and the noise level. If possible, have someone help you determine this by standing at the opposite end of the room and talking to you. Do your voices carry? Are you easily heard and understood? Do you require a sound system? You don't want to have to shout your booktalks. In addition, how easily can you hear someone talking in the audience? Are there other noise factors that could interfere with your presentation, such as street traffic, heavy equipment, airplanes, train whistles, and so on? Knowing about these in advance will help you plan accordingly. The audience can't enjoy your booktalks if they can't hear them.

Seating

What kinds of chairs are being used? Are they comfortable? Can they be moved around as needed? Are there enough of them? Discuss the seating arrangements with the event coordinator to make sure they will be arranged appropriately before you arrive. Sometimes the seating arrangements cannot be changed, such as when your presentation is part of a larger program. It is possible, however, to minimize certain problems with a little preplanning. If the seats are uncomfortable, start your presentation by incorporating some audience participation. Have the audience stand up to sing a song or repeat a phrase in unison—anything to give them a break from sitting too long.

Stage

Is there a stage? If there is, look it over carefully to see how it is accessed and how it sits in relation to the audience. Is the audience so close that they seem to be on top of you—or are they too far away to establish any intimacy? Is the stage elevated to allow better visibility? Is it large enough to allow movement and accommodate props? Get up on the stage and get a feel for it. You want to make sure the stage is secure and stable and that you feel very comfortable there.

Size

Size does matter, especially when considering how the space relates to the number of people in the audience. Too many or too few people may make the situation uncomfortable. If there are too many people for the size of the room, see if chairs can be added or the venue changed to a larger room. If there are too few people for the size of the room, try to block off a section of seating or remove some of the seating in order to concentrate the audience in a smaller area.

SOLO VERSUS PARTNER PRESENTATIONS

Whether to work alone or with someone else is one of the first decisions you'll have to make when planning your program. There are several advantages to working with someone else. For one thing, the program will require less of a time commitment, since you will be responsible for fewer booktalks than you would if you were working alone. Secondly, it's more fun to work with someone else—provided you get along with that person. Not only do you share the workload, you share everything about the experience. Working with someone allows for the option of skits, makes banter and segues easier, and takes some of the pressure off because you're not performing by yourself.

Choosing your partner is very important. Make sure to select someone who is as committed to the project as you are, with whom you work well, and whose presentation and work styles complement yours. Are you going to have an equal partnership, or are you looking for an assistant to play a supporting role? It has been our experience that an equal partnership works best and is better received by the audience. Equal partnerships require trust, simply because you're giving up total control of the program and must depend upon your partner(s) to provide input into all areas of the presentation: the number of booktalks, the kinds of books that will be discussed, the use of props and/or skits, and the amount of time allotted. In addition, you must be able to trust your partner(s) not to be scene-stealers, to uphold their part of the program, to learn their lines, and to be willing to practice as needed. The last thing you need when faced with an upcoming program is to worry about whether a partner will get cold feet and abandon you.

Although each of us has done numerous booktalk programs solo, when given the choice, we advocate team booktalking. Not only does the audience respond well to the interaction between two or more people having fun on stage, but your partner(s) will prove to be your best resource for improving the presentation. You can bounce ideas off each other, get honest feedback on a booktalk, and have fun developing an effective program. Also, your partner(s) will honestly tell you whether that prop hat looks stupid or adds the perfect touch. It's much easier to act silly in front of a whole roomful of people if you're doing it with a friend instead of standing there all alone.

PROPS AND SKITS

Anything and everything can be a prop in a booktalking program. One prop you should always use in each and every booktalk is a clean, visually appealing copy of each book you are talking about. People will want to see the book so they know what to look for—and, let's face it, to decide whether or not the book appeals to them. We *do* judge a book by its cover. We discussed the use of props in a booktalk in chapter 3; here we want to discuss incorporating booktalks using props into your overall program. Moderation is the key. An entire program that consists of only one type of booktalk, the prop booktalk, is both overwhelming and distracting. If you use too many props, the booktalk will be interrupted while you reach for the next item and the book will be lost in the prop shuffle.

Skits, however, can be used to tie the booktalks together. A skit opening the program can present the theme, provide audience participation, and set the mood as the audience anticipates the entertainment to come. A skit at the end can provide closure and neatly tie up the program, leaving the audience with a sense of completion. Another alternative, which we have used often, is to weave the skit and the booktalks together, making the booktalks a part of the skit. For example, our chillers booktalking program is a skit in which two friends gather for a sleepover to watch scary movies. When the power goes out, they decide to tell each other about scary books instead. We did this program dressed in pajamas, robes, and fuzzy slippers and laughed along with the audience when we just happened to have the scary books with us when the lights went out. We arranged in advance for the event coordinator to dim the lights at the appropriate time and to turn the lights back up at the end.

Skits cannot be done halfway. All the booktalkers need to be 100 percent committed and comfortable. Good acting is not a prerequisite, but you have to be willing to go all out. By this we mean that you have to dress appropriately, be silly, stay in character, and have fun! Even if a joke falls flat, even if you miss a line or two, even if you drop a prop, keep going. The audience will appreciate your creativity and effort.

Practicing the booktalks with skits and props is just as important as practicing the booktalks by themselves. If you're doing a program with a partner, practice the program with your partner. If you're using a skit throughout the program, practice the skit including the booktalks, so that you're comfortable with them as a cohesive unit. Every time you practice a prop booktalk, you should use the prop so that it becomes second nature. Practice is the key to a successful booktalking program and it is never as important as when you're adding elements such as props and skits.

BOOKTALK ORDER

The order in which the books are presented in a program is very important. You want to take the audience on a journey, so the order needs to enhance the mood and flow of the presentation. Just as a booktalk has a beginning that attracts attention, a middle that builds to a climax, and an ending that leaves people satisfied and yet wanting more, your whole presentation should have these same elements. The booktalks should fit together; they need to flow so that one leads to another seamlessly. Start your presentation with a shorter booktalk, one that showcases an unusual plot or character, to attract the audience's attention. The next booktalk needs to have something in common with the first—the same genre, a similar locale, or even a time frame that can be used as a segue to tie the two titles together. The transitions between booktalks need to flow so that the audience is carried along smoothly instead of being jerked from one booktalk to another. Vary your booktalk styles to keep the program moving and to maintain the interest of the audience. Your last booktalk should be your most memorable or most powerful so that the audience is left with that "wow" factor—knowing that the journey is complete, but wishing it weren't.

Two elements that are important in building a successful program are the number of booktalks and the length of the overall presentation. If you are doing a program alone and it consists of straight booktalks with no skits, props, or other discussion, the length should not exceed five or six booktalks, or about fifteen to twenty minutes. If your program incorporates a skit, props, or a partner, the program could run quite a bit longer—perhaps as long as forty-five minutes to an hour, but the variety of elements makes it entertaining enough to hold the audience's attention.

PRESENTATION SKILLS

Presentation skills are the final and most important part of the process. No matter now well your booktalks are written and your program put together, it won't be successful if your presentation skills are lacking. Here are a few public speaking fundamentals to remember as you prepare for your program:

1. Learning the Booktalk
   There's nothing more boring than watching a person read a booktalk he or she has taped to the back of the book. Take the time to learn your booktalk! It doesn't have to be perfectly memorized, but you should know it so well that you feel comfortable with it and it comes across naturally and without effort.
2. Practice
   Practice the booktalk, practice the props, practice the skits, practice the timing—practice the entire program. Practice until you feel you can handle anything that may happen during the presentation—a fire drill, an unexpected prop failure, or a burst of laughter from the audience when you least expect it. Practice doesn't mean perfection, but it does mean success.
3. Enunciation
   You want your audience to hear and understand you, so make sure your words are loud and clear. Use a sound system if needed. Choose your words so as to eliminate tongue twisters and vagueness.
4. Modulation
   Varying your tone and pitch is a good way to maintain the audience's attention throughout your presentation. An effective way to do this is to use a variety of booktalk styles.
5. Volume
   It is important to be loud enough to be heard by your audience, but varying your volume is also an excellent tool to add drama and emphasis to your presentation. Use of a stage whisper or a sudden shout can refocus the audience's attention with just a word.

6. Eye Contact

Using eye contact connects you to your audience. When you look at them, they see that you're engaged with them and focused on them. This enables them to become more involved with your words and message.

7. Gestures

Gestures are a wonderful way to provide emphasis to your presentation, but don't overuse them. Vary their use to make sure you're not doing the same thing repeatedly. Practice them to make sure they look natural.

8. Physical Presence

Use your energy and presence to take control of the stage. Act like you belong there and that you're excited to be there, even if you're nervous and scared. Show confidence through posture and movement. Don't slouch or hide behind anything. Move around the stage—make it yours.

9. Comfort Level

Comfort comes with experience. If you don't have experience, the fastest and most effective way to increase your comfort level is with practice. We can't stress this enough. It's like the old saying, "How do you get to Carnegie Hall? Practice!"

10. Book Title and Author

Every booktalk *must* include the book title and the name of the author. You could say it at the beginning or the end of the booktalk, but be sure to mention it and show the book.

11. Trial Run

When you feel your presentation is ready for an audience, do a trial run. Invite a few of your colleagues or friends to watch your program. Ask them to give you honest feedback on your timing, flow, and other presentation skills. Don't get hurt or defensive; use these comments to improve your program before you perform it in front of an audience.

12. Audience Rapport

The rapport you build with the audience is the most rewarding and fulfilling aspect of booktalking. Whether it's getting their undivided attention throughout the program, or being surrounded by them after it's over, knowing you've made that connection makes all the work worthwhile.

There are numerous books available to improve public speaking skills. We have listed just a few in the "Further Reading" section at the end of the book.

5

Publicity and Promotion

Once you have your program put together, it's time to promote your services to the community and to publicize upcoming presentations. Publicity is often overlooked, but it is an integral part of the success of any program. You must rely on publicity and promotion to generate an audience; people can't attend your program if they don't know about it. Before embarking on a publicity campaign for a program being held outside the library, however, check with the venue or event coordinator to make sure that outsiders are welcome. If the program is for the venue or host organization's members only and closed to the public, outside publicity will be pointless and potentially embarrassing.

Once you have received permission, there are several sure methods to publicize your program. These include press releases, flyers, posters, and calendars.

PRESS RELEASES

The press release is the easiest and least expensive way to reach a large number of people. Radio and television stations are required by FCC regulations to donate a portion of their airtime to public service announcements. Newspapers usually have community sections that are used to highlight local events and programs. Developing a rapport with media contacts is essential, as they are often bombarded with publicity requests. If you have good media contacts, it may help your programs receive the desired attention. Make some phone calls to local media outlets and ask to speak to the community relations liaisons. Invite them to the library, or just chat over the phone. Explain what you're trying to accomplish and ask for their assistance. Ask them for their specific font, format, and deadline requirements. This is important. If they can depend on you for snappy and concise press releases, delivered in the correct format and on time, it will make their job easier and will move your program to the top of their list. In addition, they may think of you first when looking for a library or human interest story, which will enable you to publicize your library in another context.

Press releases usually follow a set format. They must be as succinct as possible. This is not the place for flowery or descriptive language. You want to answer the five questions: who, what, when, where, and why (and you can sometimes skip the "why"). The heading of the press release will have the name of the program and the run period—that is, the time span in which you would like the press release to run. The first sentence should include the name, date, and place of the program. The second sentence should provide registration and age requirements, if applicable. The next part could give information about the speaker, if desired, or a short history of the program. Lastly, provide a contact name and phone number in case anyone needs more information about the program. See figure 5.1 for a sample press release.

FLYERS AND POSTERS

Flyers and posters are usually produced in-house. They should be colorful, appealing, and easy to read. Using different fonts can be fun, but don't get

Figure 5.1. Sample Press Release

For Release April 29, 2007
Contact: Larry Librarian
City Library
999-555-1234
Larry.Librarian@citylibrary.org

Booktalk Program at City Library

The public is invited to hear booktalks by City Library fiction specialist Larry Librarian on Saturday, May 24, at 2 p.m. in the Main Meeting Room. This event is free and open to teens and adults ages 12 and older. The theme of the booktalk program is "Mysteries to Sink Your Teeth Into"; it will feature titles in the culinary mystery genre. In addition, refreshments featuring some of the books' recipes will be served.

For more information, contact Larry Librarian at 999-555-1234.

carried away and use too many styles and sizes. The general rule is to use no more than three different fonts per flyer or poster. Use a font that can be easily read; posters should have fonts that are large enough to be read from a distance. Graphics are also a nice addition. When designing your flyers and posters, keep it simple. People don't want to read an entire page of information. They want "just the facts, ma'am." Keep it to the four main points: who, what, when, and where. If you don't have an in-house graphics specialist, flyers are easy to create on most word-processing programs. If you don't have a color printer, copying your flyer onto color paper is just as effective— but take care not to use dark colors that make reading the flyer difficult. Posters, however, usually need to be created using professional software and printed on special equipment. You can also make posters by hand on tag board, if you have some artistic ability and the results look neat and professional.

Once you've created your posters and flyers, it's time to distribute them. First of all, place them in strategic places throughout the library and venue, if the program is off-site. Second, post flyers or posters at local businesses, parks, and recreation and senior centers in your community. Be sure to leave your name and phone number in case they run out and need a new supply. Third, mailing lists can provide a distribution resource—send flyers to the names on the list with a special invitation to attend.

CALENDARS AND NEWSLETTERS

Many organizations publish calendars of events and/or newsletters. Do some research on organizations in your community. Find out the requirements for posting programs, including copy length, deadlines, and contact person. Although many organizations will include your program only if it's conducted at their site, some publicize all community events and will publish your notice if asked. One example of this is local homeowner's associations, which will often include items of interest to the people in their neighborhood. Don't forget your own library's calendar of events.

OUTREACH

There are two main methods of outreach when booktalking. One is to go outside the library and present at a specific venue. The other is to stay in the library but promote the event to a particular audience. Both methods are effective in reaching out to people who don't normally visit the library. There are many outside organizations and associations in the community looking for informative and/or entertaining programs to offer their members.

Usually they have little or no budget and would be interested in hearing about a free program that promotes books, reading, and libraries to their members. It never hurts to ask—and you may be pleasantly surprised at the enthusiastic reception you receive from an organization you thought would be uninterested.

PROMOTING LIBRARY SERVICES

A booktalking presentation is the perfect opportunity to inform the audience about the library and its services. You should bring informational brochures and handouts to each program and make sure you are equipped to answer basic questions about the library. Often audience members will surprise you with specific questions about an aspect of the library you are not familiar with or prepared to discuss. For example, Kellie visited a Kiwanis Club meeting to booktalk recent best-sellers. Afterward, someone asked her about the library's budget, and she had no idea about the specific numbers

---

Possible Booktalking Venues and Audiences

- Kiwanis clubs
- retirement communities
- bookstores
- homeowner's associations
- in-house library programs
- literacy programs
- soroptimist clubs
- book festivals
- senior centers
- library conferences and workshops
- community events
- church groups
- reading clubs
- teacher in-service days
- chambers of commerce
- special interest clubs
- holiday programs
- school family nights
- bookmobile stops

requested—nor did she want to enter into a discussion about current budget woes. Some statistics might have helped her avoid a difficult situation.

Library information can be broken down into four main categories: general information, circulation policies and statistics, special programs, and special collections.

General Information

- number of branches
- locations
- phone numbers
- hours
- number of staff members
- overall budget numbers
- personnel budget
- materials budget
- volunteers
- contact list
- Internet policies

Circulation Policies and Statistics

- library card requirements (age, residency, ID, etc.)
- checkout limit
- checkout length
- fines/fees
- renewal policies (in person, by phone, online)
- hold/reserve policies
- circulation statistics (annually, children's, etc.)
- age restrictions
- payment/amnesty policies

Special Services

- ESL tutoring/testing
- literacy services
- GED classes/testing
- computer classes
- talking book program (Library for the Blind)
- notary services
- bus passes
- translation services
- faxing

- résumés
- typewriters/word processors
- listening/viewing centers
- tours
- library programming
- cooperative learning with local schools
- obituary searching
- educator benefits (special circulation privileges for teachers)

Special Collections

- foreign language
- genealogy
- maps
- Braille
- business
- large type
- local history
- government documents
- art
- young adult
- rental collection
- parenting
- picture file
- toybrary

No one expects you to know everything about your library off the top of your head, but providing handouts and having a basic knowledge of your library's collections and services will help you look prepared in front of an audience. Remember that you can always refer audience members with questions to the appropriate staff member or follow up with them after the program.

With a little bit of preparation and research, publicity and promotion can turn out to be one of the easiest and cheapest ways to reach out into the community, capture the interest of non–library users, and introduce the library and its services to the audience. Developing a cooperative relationship with local media outlets and personnel, creating an arsenal of press releases, flyers, and posters, and knowing your library facts will provide you with the basis for effectively publicizing and promoting all your booktalk presentations.

6

Practical Matters

You're all ready to go. You have your booktalks written, your program is put together, and you're booked into a venue. You've practiced your presentations until you are thoroughly prepared and you've publicized the program in newspapers and with flyers. You're all set, right? Well . . . almost. There are a few tips that will help to ensure a smooth and trouble-free outcome. We'll call these "practical matters." The easiest way to discuss these is to just list them, in no particular order.

WHAT TO BRING TO THE PROGRAM

1. booklists—a complete list of all the titles that will be booktalked, including authors and annotations
2. props
3. books—a clean, attractive copy of each title to show the audience (no rebinds!)
4. notes/booktalks—for last-minute review
5. paper and pen—to jot down notes or to take down information
6. tape—for an emergency mending or repair job
7. water
8. badge or name tag
9. business cards
10. information about the library—handouts, statistics, and so on (see chapter 5)
11. helper—an assistant could come in handy to help distribute flyers, to direct audience traffic, or to handle props

WHAT TO WEAR

Unless you need to wear a special costume for a skit or are required to wear a uniform, keep your booktalking clothes cool and comfortable. Cool and comfortable clothing will help you feel at ease on stage and allow for easy movement. At the same time, you are representing your library, so you must present a professional image. Avoid tight-fitting, short, low-cut, too casual, or garish clothing. Also remember that you will most likely be on your feet for a length of time, so wear comfortable and appropriate shoes. Try on your outfit at home before the program to make sure you feel and look your best.

WHAT TO DO WHEN YOU ARRIVE

1. Check in
   a. Let the event coordinator know you've arrived
   b. Get last-minute changes and instructions
   c. Find out your place in the program order
   d. Find out how to get an audience count for statistics
2. Check facilities
   a. lighting
   b. sound
   c. seating arrangements
   d. staging
   e. handout table
3. Introductions
   a. Who's doing them and how?
   b. It's not a bad idea to write your own brief introduction and have it ready for the coordinator to use. Include your name, title, library name, and credentials.

YOU'RE ON!

1. Bring materials to the stage
2. Set up props
3. Put books in proper order
4. Have note cards handy
5. Take a swig of water and a deep breath
6. Smile

NOW THAT YOU'RE FINISHED . . .

1. Answer questions from the audience
2. Gather materials and sit down

3. Listen to other presentations, if applicable
4. Mingle with audience after program
5. Pass out business cards for future contacts and possible programs
6. Get audience attendance statistics from program coordinator

WHAT TO DO WHEN YOU GET
BACK TO THE LIBRARY

1. Create a display of books talked
2. Put out a supply of booklists at the service desks
3. Write a thank-you note to the event coordinator
4. Follow up on any questions that were asked at the program
5. Do a program evaluation for your records and for library administration
6. Submit statistics to administrator

Finally, figures 6.1 and 6.2 are checklists that you might find useful as an *aide memoire* in preparing a booktalk program. After using them a time or two, you can modify them to suit your own needs.

Figure 6.1. Booktalking Program Checklist

Program Information

Name of Program: _____

Date: _____ Start Time: _____

Location: _____

Address: _____

Mapquest Map Attached? ☐ Yes ☐ No ☐ Not Applicable

Contact Person's Name: _____

Title: _____ Phone Number: _____

Time Allotted for Presentation: _____

Theme/Subject Matter Requested: _____

Thank-You Note Written ☐ Yes Date Mailed: _____

Publicity Checklist

Flyers/Posters Made ☐ Yes Date Distributed: _____

Press Release Written ☐ Yes Date Sent Out: _____

Press Release Sent to:

☐ Newspapers ☐ Radio Stations ☐ Television Stations ☐ Venue
☐ Calendar ☐ Other _____

Packing Checklist

☐ Books ☐ Booklists ☐ Badge/Name Tag ☐ Booktalks/Notes
☐ Business Cards ☐ Handouts about Library ☐ Paper and Pen
☐ Props ☐ Tape ☐ Water

Figure 6.2. Booktalking Program Room Checklist

Venue Address: _____

Room Number: _____ Room Location: _____

Date Visited: _____

Room Size: ☐ Small (Seats 25 or less) ☐ Medium (Seats 26–50)
☐ Large (Seats 51–100) ☐ Extra Large (Seats 100 plus)

Seating: ☐ Fixed ☐ Movable ☐ Cushioned ☐ Folding
☐ Enough for expected audience
☐ Too few for expected audience
☐ Too many for expected audience
☐ Additional seating available ☐ Yes ☐ No
☐ Able to block off extra seating ☐ Yes ☐ No

Room Temperature: ☐ Perfect ☐ Warm ☐ Cold
Temperature is adjustable for program ☐ Yes ☐ No

Lighting: ☐ Perfect ☐ Too Bright ☐ Too Dark
Lighting is adjustable for program ☐ Yes ☐ No

Obstructions: ☐ None ☐ Fixed ☐ Present but can be moved

Sound: A sound system is needed for the program ☐ Yes ☐ No
A sound system is available for the program ☐ Yes ☐ No
Sound system quality ☐ Excellent ☐ Fine ☐ Bring one
Microphone ☐ Stationary ☐ Hand held ☐ Lavaliere

Noise: ☐ Quiet ☐ Acceptable ☐ Room is very noisy

Stage: A stage is available ☐ Yes ☐ No
A stage is elevated ☐ Yes ☐ No
A stage is easily accessible ☐ Yes ☐ No
Stage size is: ☐ Perfect ☐ Too Small ☐ Too Large
Audience location: ☐ Perfect ☐ Too Close ☐ Too Far Away

I have discussed my concerns with:
Name: _____
Title: _____ Phone: _____
Date: _____ Time: _____

I need to follow up with:
Name: _____
Title: _____ Phone: _____
Date: _____ Time: _____

7

Sample Booktalks

Now that you've studied the book and learned all about the importance of booktalking and how to create booktalks, you are ready to put together a program. This is often a daunting task, especially for a beginner. To help you, we have provided eighty-eight sample booktalks covering eleven genres. Each sample is complete with bibliographic information and a list of genres the book can be used with. Please note that most titles list more than one genre; this is because many books fall into more than one category.

Titles that fit into multiple genres are useful in providing variety in your presentations even if you are creating a program around a specific theme. For example, when we created a program on sea adventures, we decided to restrict the subject to historical sea adventures. While this might appear to be too limiting and result in a boring program, this was not the case. In order to provide the audience with variety we selected titles with different sub-genres. Some books dealt with pirates, others with war. Some were riveting tales of survival and others told of exploration and discovery. We included a story about a young, naive cabin boy on his first journey and another about a strong, independent woman taking her last voyage.

Please feel free to use the sample booktalks in your presentations. You may use them as written or alter them to better fit your voice. In order to assist you in creating your program, we have also indexed the booktalks.

CHILLERS

Definition: Books that fall into this genre literally give us chills. They play with our mind or leave us wondering; they are often disturbing, dark, and dangerous, and usually deal with issues of fear, obsession, the supernatural, or revenge. Chillers are sometimes referred to as horror stories or thrillers. Although both provide the reader with goose bumps and frights, for our purpose, a chiller is less graphic and horrific. We think of it this way: a chiller resembles an Alfred Hitchcock movie, while horror is more like Stephen King.

Purpose: Provide the reader with the opportunity to be a voyeur and safely explore the frightening world of twisted plots, obsession, revenge, madness, or the supernatural.

General Appeal Characteristics

Storylines contain many twists, surprises, dangers, and levels of fear. Readers are able to visit this nightmarish world within the safety and security of their normal lives.

Setting is vital to this genre, as it provides readers with the atmosphere needed to create impact. Accurate and consistent detail is essential in creating the right mood. Often these stories take place in a seemingly normal world that turns out to be desperately flawed.

Pacing is important in that the story must keep moving along. Although chillers can contain long descriptions necessary to create atmosphere, the plot must be compelling enough to keep readers engrossed. Mind games are a larger component than physical action in this genre. Although many chillers depict physical battles, they are life-and-death struggles, not macho posturings.

Characters are crucial to this genre and often fall into one or more of three categories: misfit, innocent, or villain. Misfits are usually sympathetic and often bear the brunt of the villain's actions. They can be different physically, mentally, or emotionally. They can be a member of a different society, race, gender, age, or species, or have an illness, either mental or physical, that sets them apart. *Misfits* can be innocents, but sometimes they turn into villains as a result of constant torment or circumstances beyond their control. Innocents are characters that readers are most likely to relate to. They often stumble into a nightmarish world that they are dreadfully unprepared for. *Innocents* either find the strength to prevail or meet their demise. *Villains* are usually the most dramatic characters. The variety of traits that can be attributed to them seems endless. Villains can be human or not, real or imaginary characters; they can be sane or suffer from uncontrollable madness. The one characteristic all villains share is the ability to do evil, or cause harm to other characters. The story line usually revolves around the villain and his or her interaction with one or more other characters.

Samples

The Mind Game by Hector MacDonald
New York: Ballantine, 2001
Chiller

It all started innocently enough. Ben originally didn't want to get involved in the experiment, but when his new girlfriend heard about it, she persuaded him to give it a go. Ben had to admit it did sound wonderful: a full two weeks on an African beach, every care provided for, every want satisfied—all provided as part of the experiment. And all he had to do was have a small monitoring device implanted into the back of his skull and keep a journal of his emotions.

Yes, it all started innocently enough. But soon bad things started happening, like an airplane losing control and Ben's being arrested on a drug charge—and then Ben can't keep track of what's supposed to be part of the experiment and what isn't. Is he being manipulated without his control just to monitor his wild swing of emotions? Or is the whole thing just a front for his professor's new game theory? Every time Ben thinks he knows the next move, he finds another layer of deception and another person to distrust, until he feels as if he's going mad. Or is that also part of the plan? *The Mind Game* by Hector MacDonald.

*   *   *

24/7 by Jim Brown
New York: Ballantine, 2001
Chiller

Dana Kirsten needs a break. A single mother who works three jobs just to make ends meet, she is faced with unending medical bills as her daughter, Jenna, fights a severe form of muscular dystrophy.

Then Dana hears about a new reality TV program called *24/7*. Twelve people will be dropped off on an uninhabited island in the Caribbean filled with hidden cameras that allow the public to watch them by satellite or over the Internet twenty-four hours a day, seven days a week. Challenges will have to be faced, and every three days the viewing public will vote off one contestant. The winner will receive $2 million and his or her heart's desire.

"Just do what you have to do." That's what Dana's father always said. She knew what she had to do. She had to get on *24/7*; she had to win, this one time; and she had to catch a break.

However, once on the island, live TV turns into death TV as the show is taken over by a madman who has murdered the crew and infected the contestants with a designer virus that eats human flesh . . . from the inside out.

Isolated and terrified, the contestants struggle to survive as the producers watch in helpless horror. When military ships are spotted from the island,

Dana is sure help has come at last—but she soon realizes how wrong she is. The ships are there not to rescue them but to make sure no one leaves the island to spread the deadly virus to the rest of the world.

The challenges are now deadly and when the public votes they're no longer voting someone off the island; they are choosing the contestant they want to watch die—in *24/7*, a debut novel by Jim Brown.

                              *   *   *

Five Mile House by Karen Novak
New York: Bloomsbury, 2000
Chiller, Mystery
Everyone knows Five Mile House is haunted. One hundred years ago Eleanor Bly murdered her seven children and then committed suicide. For one hundred years Eleanor Bly's name has been synonymous with murder and madness. For one hundred years she has been waiting to tell the terrible truth of what happened that night.

Now Leslie Stone has come to Five Mile House, and Eleanor hopes her torment will finally end. But Leslie has ghosts of her own. She's haunted by the voice of a little girl brutally raped and murdered; haunted by the face of the suspect she shot in cold blood; haunted by the label "psycho cop."

Can these two damaged souls reach each other through one hundred years of death? Can they work together to uncover and stop the evil that lives in Five Mile House? *Five Mile House* by Karen Novak.

                              *   *   *

Possession by Peter James
New York: Doubleday, 1988
Chiller
Alex Hightower is a successful literary agent in London whose life is about to undergo dramatic changes. It begins when Alex is awakened by a strange noise and is surprised to see her son Fabian standing at the foot of her bed. She asks what he's doing, but instead of answering Fabian smiles and tells her to go back to sleep and he'll see her later.

Alex leaves for work determined to finish early and spend the evening with her son. That's when her world falls apart. The police bring her the terrible news that Fabian was killed in a car accident—yesterday. Alex knows that there's been a horrible mistake, Fabian couldn't have died yesterday—she saw him; she talked to him this morning.

Alex rushes home to prove to the police that they're wrong, but when she gets there she finds no sign of Fabian. He is not home; he did not come home this morning . . . Fabian is dead.

As Alex tries to deal with the sudden death of her son, she convinces herself that she must have been dreaming when she saw Fabian at the foot of her bed. She rejects her friends' suggestion of ghosts coming back to say good-bye for one last time—until strange things start to happen. Messages from Fabian appear on Alex's computer; people she invites over start speaking to her . . . in Fabian's voice.

Fearing for her sanity, Alex contacts a psychic who tells her she is in great danger. Fabian wants to come back, but he can only do so by possessing another body . . . hers.

Now Alex is in a desperate struggle to save her son's soul before he destroys hers. *Possession* by Peter James.

*   *   *

A Winter Haunting by Dan Simmons
New York: William Morrow, 2002
Chiller

Dale Stewart was a beloved father and husband, a successful author, and a respected college professor. The definitive word is "was." Dale lost his family when he had an illicit affair with one of his graduate students; he's lost interest in his mountain men books and won't write them anymore; and he's decided to take a one-year sabbatical from his teaching job to get his life in order.

Dale has decided that his problems stem from the summer of 1960, when he was eleven years old and lost his best friend, Duane, to a horrible accident. Dale's memory of that summer is spotty at best. He feels that if he can go back to his hometown and regain the memories of that lost summer, his life will begin to make sense and he will be able to move on. He's decided that the best way to accomplish this is to move into Duane's old abandoned home. Dale has made a big mistake.

The problems begin right away. First, there's the overwhelming stench that greets Dale when he first enters the house shortly after midnight. Unable to stand the smell and sure that something has died in the house, Dale decides to sleep in the car and wait until morning to check it out. When morning comes, however, the smell is gone. Weird. Dale is also annoyed to find that his cell phone won't work anywhere on the property, which means he can't make or receive calls, his e-mail won't work, and he can't get online. How, then, is he getting messages on his computer? Even though his AOL account doesn't work, when he's out of the study, the "You've got mail" voice bellows out of the computer and he returns to find cryptic, sometimes threatening messages on the screen. And then there's the light in the upstairs window. What's the big deal? you ask. Well, the second floor doesn't have any electricity and it's been sealed off for more than fifty years. Where is the light coming from? Who or what is making the scratching noises from inside the old coal bin? And where did the black dogs come from—the ones that follow Dale when he goes for a walk then seem to disappear into thin air?

Forty-one years after Duane's death, Dale Stewart moved into his house
. . . it's going to be a very long, horrifying winter in *A Winter Haunting* by
Dan Simmons.

✻   ✻   ✻

Second Sight by Beth Amos
New York: HarperCollins, 1998
Chiller, Mystery

Marlie Kaplan used to be a crackerjack investigative reporter, but a terrible
accident left her permanently blind. Then an experimental surgical procedure restored part of her eyesight. She still can't see very well, but soon she
discovers that the procedure has left her with the ability to sense things other
people can't see. She may not be able to make out faces too well, but she can
see halos of light and colors that surround people and reveal their intentions
and personalities.

When Marlie's partner is killed, Marlie is the only witness to the murder,
but her blindness guarantees her safety. Her special sight, however, makes
her suspect one person as the murderer. Does she dare reveal her suspicions
based on her perceptions? She could warn others, but she doubts they would
believe her. Is Marlie right about the identity of the murderer, or is she still
blind to what's in front of her very own eyes until it's almost too late to save
herself? Marlie's hesitation about what's right in front of her own eyes could
be her own undoing in *Second Sight* by Beth Amos.

✻   ✻   ✻

Belladonna by Karen Moline
New York: Warner, 1998
Chiller

Something very bad happened to Belladonna once. Something very, very
bad. She used to be Isabella Ariel Nickerson, an eighteen-year-old from
Minnesota, a sweet and trusting girl. Then she went to London to visit her
cousin and was invited to a party, a very special party at which she was the
guest of honor. A party at which the guest of honor was auctioned off to
one lucky member of the club—to be his personal slave for as long as he
wanted.

You can only imagine the unspeakable horrors Isabella was exposed to
during the many years she was held in captivity by His Lordship, the only
name she had for her captor. When she finally escaped, she knew she could
no longer remain Isabella, so she invented a new name for herself: Belladonna. Belladonna, the pretty poisonous flower who lives for one thing:
revenge. She has the money, she has the time, and she has the help of all the
people she needs to find the man who robbed her of her freedom and dignity. And she won't rest until she finds him. *Belladonna* by Karen Moline.

* * *

In the Lake of the Woods by Tim O'Brien
Boston: Houghton Mifflin, 1994
Chiller, Mystery

John and Kathy Wade have come to the small lake deep in Minnesota's north woods to recover and heal from a terrible blow: John's lost election bid for senator. As the two try to understand what happened, they begin to examine their own relationship to try to figure out what went wrong in their marriage.

Then one morning John wakes up and Kathy is gone. At first he thinks that perhaps she has gone for a walk, or taken the boat out, or even left him. But soon it becomes apparent that Kathy has just disappeared, and John himself is under suspicion. As the narrator of the story begins to unravel the truth, much deception comes to light. Who is John? What really happened when he was in Vietnam? Why does he remember some things about the night before Kathy's disappearance that he chooses not to tell the police?

Tim O'Brien weaves together interviews, police interrogations, and media speculation to create this riveting, often unsettling mystery. *In the Lake of the Woods* by Tim O'Brien.

GENERAL FICTION

Definition: These are novels that don't quite fit into any specific genre. They are unusual stories whose major story line can't be assigned any one category, although they may have subplots or minor story lines that fit into a genre.

Purpose: Provide the reader with an interesting reading experience that defies being pigeonholed.

General Appeal Characteristics

These novels are usually unique or quirky in some way. They may have a different view on a common subject or be so original that none of the existing genres can be applied.

Provides the reader with something different. These are the books that you read and enjoy, but when someone asks you what they're about you find it difficult to answer and usually end up saying "It's hard to explain, but just read it . . . you'll love it."

Could be the exciting beginning of a whole new genre.

Samples

The Time Traveler's Wife by Audrey Niffenegger
San Francisco: MacAdam/Cage, 2003
General Fiction, Romance

When Clare and Henry meet for the first time, Clare has actually known Henry for many years. Henry started visiting Clare when she was a little girl, so she has grown up knowing her future husband. At first she was a little afraid of the man who would suddenly appear, naked, in the middle of her back yard, but she soon grew to expect the unexpected when it came to Henry. After all, you can't have a normal life if you're married to a time traveler.

When Clare and Henry meet for the first time, Henry has never seen Clare before in his life. At first he is a little taken aback by this person who screams his name and practically knocks him over with a huge hug, but then he figures out she's from his future and he might as well get used to her. Henry has been traveling around time since he was four years old and things haven't been normal for him for a long time.

Romeo and Juliet, move over. Another great couple has joined the ranks of literary true love. Henry and Clare may have an unconventional life together, but this remarkable story of their devotion to each other will convince you that their love will truly stand the test of time. *The Time Traveler's Wife* by Audrey Niffenegger.

*   *   *

Coyote Cowgirl by Kim Antieau
New York: Forge, 2003
General Fiction, Humor, Women's Fiction

Jeanne Les Flambeaux is a failure. Not only that, she's a failure in a family that's been made of overachievers for generations. They are known as the great chefs of the Southwest. Her parents own and operate a very successful restaurant in Scottsdale, Arizona.

Jeanne can't cook. In fact, she can't do much of anything. It seems that she either breaks or screws up everything she touches. As Jeanne herself says, she's an idiot savant . . . if you drop the savant part.

So she isn't *really* surprised at her latest fiasco, although this may be the biggest mistake of her life. You see, Jeanne was given only one job for the big family celebration: put the family heirlooms back in the safe when the celebration was over. Of course she forgot, and now they've been stolen.

Determined to recover the stolen objects before her parents discover they're missing, Jeanne begins a quest that takes her across the American Southwest. Her only help is a crystal skull that talks only to her and calls himself Crane.

Coyote Cowgirl, a funny, touching, intriguing novel by Kim Antieau.

✳   ✳   ✳

The Memory Keeper's Daughter by Kim Edwards
New York: Viking, 2005
General Fiction

What would you do? During a snowstorm your wife gives birth to twins, a boy and a girl. The boy is strong and healthy, but the girl has Down syndrome. You want to spare your wife the pain of raising a handicapped child, so you give the baby to your nurse to take to an institution. It will be better for the baby, you think as you hand her over; they are more equipped to handle these things. You tell your wife that the baby girl died. She names the dead baby Phoebe and you both cry at her memorial service.

What would you do? You are the nurse who must take the baby to the institution. You have always been a little in love with your employer, the doctor, and have never questioned his decisions—until you walk into that horrible place and realize there's no way you could possible leave that sweet baby there. So you take her home and pack up your things and disappear. And you name the baby Phoebe, the name her mother chose. Her baby is dead to her, but not to you. You will raise this baby as if she were your own.

What would you do? A brother and sister grow up without knowing the other. One man has a terrible secret that he cannot share with his wife, despite the fact that this secret may destroy their marriage. One mother cannot forget the pain of losing a daughter and another mother cannot bear the pain of having her secret discovered. Is there any way of making things right, or do you just go on living the same lie month after month, year after year?

What would you do? *The Memory Keeper's Daughter* by Kim Edwards.

✳   ✳   ✳

The Handmaid's Tale by Margaret Atwood
Boston: Houghton Mifflin, 1986
General Fiction, Women's Fiction

Imagine a world where women aren't allowed to hold jobs, choose their husbands, or even choose what they want to wear. A world where signs are pictures, not words; for instance, if you go to a butcher shop you won't see a sign that says "Pete's Meats"—you'll see a picture of a pork chop. This is done because this is a world where women aren't allowed to read. A world where a few men have total control and use their interpretation of the Bible to determine how everyone behaves and what everyone knows. No, I'm not talking about Afghanistan; I'm talking about the United States. Well, a United States in the future, one that's now called Gilead.

After the ravages of war and pollution caused widespread unrest and infertility, a group of powerful men called commanders have taken control. Women are valued only if they can still bear healthy children. Everything is taken from them: their homes, their children and husbands, even their names. The slightest resistance means a choice between banishment to a horrible place known as "the colonies," torture, or death. They are no longer considered to be people; they are now Handmaids, and this is their story. *The Handmaid's Tale* by Margaret Atwood.

✳   ✳   ✳

The Ha-Ha by Dave King
New York: Little, Brown, 2005
General Fiction

It isn't hard for Howard Kapostash to shut out the world. A brain injury has left him unable to communicate with anyone and a broken heart has left him unwilling to even try. Shut tight inside the walls he has made for himself, Howard is reluctant to get involved, but when Sylvia, his old high school sweetheart, asks him to take care of her son while she's in rehab, he can't say no.

It's not easy to deal with a nine-year-old child, and Howard's communication problems make things even more difficult. Howard's roommates, however, rally around Ryan and make him the center of attention. Laurel, a Vietnamese American woman from Texas, makes him homemade soup and gets him dressed for school. Nit and Nat (Howard can never remember their real names) teach Ryan baseball and take him on picnics. Before long the household is an actual family, complete with all the joys and sorrows that families bring.

Howard keeps reminding himself that the situation is only temporary, but what will happen when Sylvia comes back? For the first time in his life, Howard feels like a human being instead of a disability, and he'll do anything to keep this feeling alive—no matter what it takes. *The Ha-Ha* by Dave King.

✳   ✳   ✳

Montana, 1948 by Larry Watson
Minneapolis: Milkweed Editions, 1993
General Fiction, Historical Fiction

It was a summer David Hayden can't forget. The summer of 1948, the summer he was twelve years old. The summer his world fell apart.

It was supposed to be a normal summer, one that involved getting his chores done as early as possible so he could play until dark; a carefree summer full of friends, adventures, and lazy days.

But things weren't what they seemed in tiny Bentrock, Montana. David's father, Wesley, was sheriff of the town. Wesley Hayden never wanted to be sheriff; he went to school to be a lawyer, but he inherited the job from his father, an overbearing man who wouldn't take no for an answer.

David's uncle Frank was Wesley's older brother, a war hero and the town's most respected doctor.

Marie Little Soldier, a proud, statuesque Sioux, was the Haydens' housekeeper. It all began when Marie got sick but begged David's parents not to take her to Uncle Frank.

What was the horrifying connection between these three people? That's what haunts David's memory, even forty years later. David is an adult now, but the events of that summer are as fresh and frightening now as they were then.

Montana, 1948 by Larry Watson, a powerful story of love, justice, and family loyalty.

* * *

The Memory of Running by Ron McLarty
New York: Viking, 2005
General Fiction

Smithy Ide knows he's a loser. He's an alcoholic and smokes too much. He's overweight and has no friends. And he works in a toy action figure factory, making sure all the arms and legs are properly attached. Yes, things can't get much worse for Smithy—or so he thinks, until the week both his parents die in a car accident and he learns that his sister, Bethany, is in the Los Angeles morgue.

Smithy always thought he had a great childhood. But between the ball games, picnics, and family vacations, there was tension in the family because of Bethany and her mental illness. Despite the drama, Smithy dearly loves his sister, and the thought of her lying all alone waiting for someone to come get her fills him with a terrible sadness.

The night after his parents' funeral, Smithy sits on his old Raleigh bicycle in the garage and thinks about his pathetic life. It could be the enormous stress he was under, or it could be the six-pack of beer he just drank, but right there and then Smithy decides he is going to ride that bike all the way to L.A. and bring his sister home for good. It doesn't matter to him that he weighs 279 pounds. It doesn't matter that he'll have to quit his job. It doesn't even matter that he hasn't ridden a bike in thirty years and isn't sure he remembers how. The only thing that matters is family, and right now, Bethany needs him more than ever before. *The Memory of Running* by Ron McLarty.

* * *

The Inn at Lake Devine by Elinor Lipman
New York: Random House, 1998
General Fiction, Multicultural

"Thank you for your inquiry but guests who feel most comfortable here, and return year after year, are Gentiles." Thirteen-year-old Natalie Marx couldn't believe what she was reading. Did her mother *really* get that response to her letter inquiring about rates and dates of availability for the Inn at Lake Devine? Experiencing her first taste of blatant anti-Semitism shocks Natalie and she becomes obsessed with staying at the inn, and meeting the bigoted family that owns and operates it.

At first, Natalie bombards owner Ingrid Berry with phone calls and letters talking about Anne Frank and famous convert Elizabeth Taylor. She points out the value and honor of having the same blood as Moses, Leonard Bernstein, and Sid Caesar. She even sends the inn a copy of the Civil Rights Act, hoping to scare the Berrys into relenting for fear of prosecution under the new law. All of this proves ineffective, however, and Natalie is about to give up when she discovers that a girl she met at camp will be vacationing with her family at the inn. Natalie finagles an invitation and is delighted that she has finally outwitted the Berrys and will stay at their precious inn after all.

Once she arrives, however, Natalie finds that manipulating her way into a place she's not welcome is not as much fun as she suspected. For the next ten years Natalie's personal, professional, and romantic life becomes hopelessly entwined with the people she met and the experiences she had while spending that fateful summer at the Inn at Lake Devine. *The Inn at Lake Devine* by Elinor Lipman.

HISTORICAL FICTION

Definition: Simply put, this genre includes any novel that is set in the past. This is the most accepted definition of the genre and the one we use for our purposes. A word of warning, however: among some fans of this genre there is strong disagreement on what constitutes "the past." Some feel that the past is any period of time more than twenty-five years ago; others feel that the book must deal with a time period before the lifetime and experience of the author. For those who adhere to the second definition, Jane Austen's books would not be considered historical fiction because she wrote about the time in which she lived, even though that time has long since passed for her current readers.

Purpose: Bring history to life in novel form with respect for historical accuracy and detail.

General Appeal Characteristics
   Provides a plethora of accurate detail in characters, events, and setting. Setting can include location, culture, society, education, and so on.

Characters are well developed and, whether based on actual persons or
not, seem real and fit with the time period of the novel.

The main story line focuses on a particular period of time or event. The
period of time may be limited to a few days, months, or years, or span
numerous generations of a particular family.

Historical fiction is usually comprised of stories that unfold slowly, giving
the reader time to absorb the rich detail provided.

Samples

The Red Tent by Anita Diamant
New York: St. Martin's, 1997
Historical Fiction, Women's Fiction

It is the time of the book of Genesis, of Jacob and his twelve sons. But
Jacob had a thirteenth child, a daughter named Dinah. The Bible only hints
of her existence, a brief passage telling of her rape and the vengeance exacted
by her brothers. But there is so much more to Dinah's life, and here, for the
first time, we hear her story in her own voice.

Born of Leah but raised by all of Jacob's wives, Dinah learned how to be
a midwife from Rachel. Zilpah taught her how to think for herself. Beautiful
Leah gave her the gift of confidence, and Bilhah kept all her secrets.

Anita Diamant weaves a haunting tale that beautifully captures the flavor
of the ancient world as it takes us back to the beginning, to our most ancient
traditions: to a time of kings and caravans, shepherds and slaves, when
women were subjugated by men but persevered by bonding together, sharing
their husbands, their children, their lives. Journey back to a time when
women were tied to each other with a bind as natural as the moon and the
tides, back to the time of the red tent. *The Red Tent* by Anita Diamant.

*   *   *

Pompeii by Robert Harris
New York: Random House, 2003
Historical Fiction

Ah, what a glorious life. To have the wealth and power to be able to just
sit back and relax in your luxurious villa and enjoy the peace and beauty of
the Mediterranean coast during the hot days of summer. Oh, sure, there are
laws restricting the use of water; although Italy is surrounded on three sides
by the Mediterranean, fresh water is not plentiful and should be used sparingly. But this doesn't concern you, since everyone knows that laws are for
peasants and slaves, not for the rich and powerful citizens of the Roman
Empire.

When, for the first time in generations, the great aqueduct that brings
fresh water to the cities in the Bay of Naples begins to fail, a young engineer,

Marcus Attilius, is sent from Rome to discover and fix the problem. Despite the overwhelming burdens and obstacles caused by the empire's limitless political intrigue and corruption, Marcus finally determines that the problem lies at the root of the aqueduct, high atop Mount Vesuvius.

Sure that there has been a break in the line, Marcus and his crew set off to begin repairs, never suspecting the cataclysmic destruction they are about to face.

Set in a four-day period, here is a book so full of life, so rich in detail, that you have to be careful that your eyes and lungs don't burn from the suffocating hot ash as Robert Harris takes you back in time to the eruption of Mount Vesuvius and the destruction of Pompeii.

✳   ✳   ✳

The Illuminator by Brenda Rickman Vantrease
New York: St. Martin's, 2005
Historical Fiction, Romance

It is fourteenth-century England and a time of plagues, war, and the Protestant Reformation. Famous churchman John Wycliffe is in hiding to work on translating the Bible into English, which is against church teaching. If he or anyone helping him is caught, they will be put into prison or even executed. To illustrate his translation, he has enlisted the help of Finn, a master illuminator, who is well known to church leaders and often does work for them as a mask for his underground activities.

At this time in history, England is rife with political and social conflict between the church and the monarchy. Lady Kathryn of Blackingham Manor just lost her husband and is frantically trying to find the money to pay her taxes to the crown and her tithes to the church. In an attempt to appease the crown, she allows the local sheriff, Sir Guy, to think she may be interested in entering into a marriage contract with him. To pacify the church, she agrees to lodge Finn the Illuminator and his young daughter while he works on consignment for them.

When the local priest disappears after visiting Blackingham Manor, Kathryn finds her household under suspicion from both church and state, and she is worried that she will be forced to marry the sheriff to save her family. But as she gets to know Finn better, she finds herself attracted to him, even though he is a lowly artisan and unsuitable for an alliance. What should she do? As Kathryn debates a course of action, events take place around her that force her to choose sides, with disastrous results. *The Illuminator* by Brenda Rickman Vantrease.

✳   ✳   ✳

These Is My Words by Nancy E. Turner
New York: Regan Books, 1998
Historical Fiction, Women's Fiction

Sarah Prine is seventeen years old when her father decides to move the family from the unbearable heat of the Arizona Territory to the cooler, greener lands of southeast Texas. The year is 1881, and the journey is so fraught with peril that Sarah decides to keep a diary so that if they die on the way, whoever finds their bones will know who they were.

Written in a style as stark and beautiful as the Arizona desert itself and based on the memoirs of the author's great-grandmother, *These Is My Words* takes us back to the time of the American frontier. As Arizona develops from a desolate territory to a thriving state, Sarah grows from a frightened, barely literate teenager into the strong, wise matriarch of her family. Through Sarah's eyes, we experience the harshness of daily life and marvel at the indomitable will and courage of the pioneers who not only survived the savagely wild frontier, but conquered it in *These Is My Words*, a debut novel by Nancy Turner.

* * *

Deafening by Frances Itani
New York: Atlantic Monthly Press, 2003
Historical Fiction

Grania O'Neill lives in a world of her own. She may have a loving family and live in a busy Canadian town at the turn of the century, but she doesn't really fit in anywhere. Grania is different because she cannot talk or hear. When her family sends her far away to a school for the deaf and blind, Grania feels neglected and lonely, but she learns many things, like how to talk so that strangers can understand her and how to use sign language to communicate with her new friends. There is one special friend who becomes quite enamored with her. Jim Lloyd is a hearing man who meets this beautiful young lady and is determined to be with her, hearing or not.

Grania and Jim fall in love and marry, because they have a connection that goes beyond words. All they have to do is look at each other to know what the other is thinking. Two weeks after their wedding, however, Jim must leave his new wife. World War I is in full force and he's needed overseas. This means that Grania is again in a world of her own, only now she's a married woman who must learn to be strong—both for herself and for her new husband, whom she misses more than anything.

Will Jim make it home again? Every night he looks at Grania's picture and prays the war will end soon. Every day Grania does her volunteer work and waits to hear word of his safety. They knew their love could survive anything, but as the weeks turn into months, they wonder if they can truly survive such loneliness and longing. *Deafening* by Frances Itani.

* * *

Grand Ambition by Lisa Michaels
New York: Norton, 2001
Historical Fiction

Bessie Haley doesn't want to live in West Virginia all her life. She wants adventure and excitement, but instead she elopes to Kentucky and tries to convince herself that her life will be fine; everything will work out. It's 1926, and when most women would be happy to be married, Bessie runs away . . . on her wedding night.

While living in California, Bessie meets Glen Hyde, a strong, tender, and thoughtful man who sweeps her off her feet. Glen convinces her not only that they should get married but that they should spend their honeymoon running the rapids of the mightiest river of them all, the Colorado, as it cuts through the wild splendor of the Grand Canyon.

It is fact that Glen and Bessie Hyde began their journey in a homemade boat on October 20, 1928. It is fact that Bessie kept a diary of their trip and planned to write a book about their journey and live off the fame of being the first woman to brave the rapids of the Colorado River. It is fact that they didn't make it.

Glen and Bessie Hyde have become legend in Arizona. Although there was an extensive search and their boat was found undamaged, nothing has ever been found of them. Rumors abound of betrayal and murder, and stories are told of Bessie sightings—but the truth is that Glen and Bessie Hyde vanished without a trace.

Now, for the first time, Lisa Michaels tries to fill in the story with a fictionalized account of the journey. Based on historical documents, *Grand Ambition* tries to answer the question that has haunted the Grand Canyon for more than seventy-five years: What happened to Glen and Bessie Hyde?

*   *   *

The Keeper's Son by Homer Hickam
New York: Thomas Dunne, 2003
Historical Fiction

The lighthouse on Killakeet Island has been under the care of the Thurlow family for three generations. One day when Josh Thurlow was fourteen years old, his father decided to leave him in charge while he made a day trip to another island. It was a big responsibility for Josh—not only did he have to light the lanterns at exactly the right time, he had to watch his two-year-old brother, Jacob. The day was long, but Josh handled everything okay—until he saw a pretty little boat bobbing about on the waves. It should have been easy to bring in, but a terrible thing happened: Somehow Jacob crawled into it and strong winds carried the baby away, never to be seen or heard from again.

Now it is twenty years later, and Josh finds himself back on Killakeet

Island, a place that for him is filled with guilt and remorse. But he's not on the island to keep the lighthouse. He's on the island as the commander of the *Maudie Jane*, a Coast Guard boat assigned to protect the island during World War II. Little does anyone, including Josh, suspect that German U-boats have been traveling up and down the Eastern seaboard and are planning to attack Killakeet Island. Can Josh's small crew defend the whole island against a force of German submarines? Josh failed once before to save a life; this time he's determined to make up for it by saving a whole town. *The Keeper's Son* by Homer Hickam.

* * *

The Final Confession of Mabel Stark by Robert Hough
New York: Atlantic Monthly Press, 2003
Historical Fiction

Come one, come all to the greatest show on earth! Please direct your attention to ring number three, where the world-famous Mabel Stark, wearing her trademark white leather jumpsuit, has her tiger act. See how courageous she is when the big cats roar at her! Watch how fearless she is as she puts them through their paces! Don't worry about Mabel—she's been mauled more times than a cat has lives, and she still comes back for more.

It was the golden age of the circus, in the early part of the twentieth century, when Mabel Stark discovered her love for tigers. After being orphaned at a young age, she was a nursing student when she met her first husband. Married life was not what she expected, however, and a nervous breakdown of sorts got her committed to a mental institution. A carnival was in town one night, and she escaped from the institution to become one of the Dancing Girls of Baghdad, a burlesque show. Eventually, after a series of dancing and daredevil acts for the Al G. Barnes Wild Animal Circus, she talked her way into learning the art of tiger training.

Mabel Stark always said, "You can't mix tigers and husbands. And anyhow, I prefer tigers." Married a total of five times, Mabel discovered that tigers make the best friends. Known for her wild ways with men and her fearless ways with tigers, Mabel looks back on a long life filled with dark secrets, broken dreams, and lost friends, and wants to set the record straight in this, her final confession. *The Final Confession of Mabel Stark* by Robert Hough.

HUMOROUS FICTION

Definition: The most basic definition of humorous fiction is a book that makes you laugh. However, we found this genre to be one of the most difficult for which to write booktalks. The reason for this is that humor is extremely personal. What one person finds to be funny, another might consider to be stupid or even offensive. Age, race, gender, culture, education, physical characteristics, and more play a role in determining what a person thinks is funny. Humorous fiction can employ a variety of elements, including quirky characters, unusual settings, funny situations, ridiculous misunderstandings, and more. Humor can be set in any time or location and can be found in most other genres.

Purpose: Provide the reader with a lighthearted reading experience, hopefully resulting in occasional bursts of laughter.

General Appeal Characteristics

These books provide quick, light reads that can easily be put down and picked up at a later time without losing the story line. They do not require readers to ponder an issue or solve a problem; readers are free to relax and enjoy. Quirky characters, unusual settings, funny situations, and so on enable the reader to escape the stress and grind of daily life.

Books are usually short in length so they don't require a large time commitment from readers.

Characters are well developed and easy for readers to relate to. Most main characters are likable people who, while silly or eccentric at times, are easily understood by the reader.

Language is easily read and understood. Passages or chapters are short and snappy; you're not going to find voluminous tomes in the humor genre.

Samples

Sister Betty! God's Calling You, Again! by Pat G'Orge Walker
New York: Dafina, 2003
Humorous Fiction, Multicultural

Pat G'Orge Walker has a hit on her hands with this hilarious collection of tales about the congregation of the Ain't Nobody Else Right But Us—All Others Goin' to Hell Church.

Beginning with the story of how Sister Betty's life was forever changed one quiet afternoon when she received a phone call from God (in the middle of her favorite soap opera) and continuing with other misadventures of this God-fearing, Bible-thumping collection of characters, you'll be hopelessly hooked.

With congregation members including the Reverend Knott Enuff Money, Sister Carrie Onn, Sister Aggie Tate, Council Man Hippo Crit, and others, you'll never want to leave the small town of Pelzer, South Carolina. *Sister Betty! God's Calling You, Again!* by Pat G'Orge Walker.

* * *

Plain Heathen Mischief by Martin Clark
New York: Knopf, 2004
Humorous Fiction

When defrocked Baptist minister Joel King is released from jail after serving a six-month sentence for statutory rape, he has no idea what he's going to do next. Being in a state of flux, he takes up an offer by Edmond, a former parishioner, to drive him from Virginia to Montana, even though his instincts warn against it. You see, ex-minister Joel King has run out of options. His wife wants a divorce, his teenage victim is suing him for $5 million, and his conviction severely limits any job prospects. Before he knows it, Joel is agreeing to help Edmond with an elaborate scheme to commit insurance fraud. Thinking this will be a victimless crime and he can use the money to help others, Joel soon finds himself with the feds, state police, and local detectives watching his every move, eager to put this ex-con back in jail.

Joel King is not immoral, all evidence to the contrary. He didn't really rape young Christy Darden, now eighteen years of age, but he did step over the line with her, and Joel King believes there is no such thing as a partial sin. As he always preached from the pulpit, "There's the straight, correct, narrow route and all the rest is just plain heathen mischief." Now a series of dubious choices has involved him in a darkly comic situation of crosses and double-crosses as he tries to do the right thing in a world gone horribly wrong. *Plain Heathen Mischief* by Martin Clark.

* * *

Practical Demonkeeping: A Comedy of Horrors by Christopher Moore
New York: St. Martin's, 1992
Humorous Fiction

Pine Cove is a sleepy tourist town on the California coast whose residents are . . . well, nuts. There's the photographer, Robert Masterson, who's also the town drunk and whose idea of cleaning up is to pile all the dirty dishes into laundry baskets and run them through the car wash. Augustus Brine is a local merchant who runs the bait, tackle, and fine wines shop and dreams of someday becoming a famous madam. Effrom Elliot is a retiree who rises at five every morning to watch the spandex-clad women on exercise programs, sure that he has found a secret porn channel. And now, there are two new characters for the residents to deal with: Travis, an ex-priest who inadvertently called forth a demon from hell and now can't get rid of him; and Catch, the demon, who is invisible to all but Travis until it's time to eat. Then he turns into a giant, scaly monster that eats humans with the same careless delight that we eat M&Ms.

If Pine Cove thought it had trouble before they're in for it now, 'cause

Travis and Catch are in town—and all hell's broken loose. *Practical Demon-keeping: A Comedy of Horrors* by Christopher Moore.

*   *   *

Eat Cake by Jeanne Ray
New York: Shaye Arehart, 2003
Humorous Fiction, Women's Fiction

Ruth loves to bake cakes. To her, cake provides all the answers—to hunger, to stress, to prayer. Whenever she needs to relax, she makes a cake. Whenever she needs to celebrate, she makes a cake. And whenever life seems to be falling apart all around her, she makes a cake.

Lately, Ruth has been making a lot of cakes. When her mother moved in after her house was burglarized, it took a goodly amount of deep breathing and German chocolate to get through each day. Then her father called from the hospital. It seems that he fell down an empty elevator shaft, broke both his wrists, and needs a place to stay. Uh-oh. Ruth's parents have been divorced for years and hate each other with a vehemence that makes any world war look like a cakewalk. It will take a double shot of political negotiation and vanilla cream to make this work. Add two children, an unemployed husband, and a feisty physical therapist, and Ruth begins to long for the past when all she had to worry about was teenage angst and what kind of frosting to use on a buttermilk walnut spice.

Got a craving for a hilarious, fun-filled romp through someone else's nightmare? Pull up a chair to the table and have a piece. *Eat Cake* by Jeanne Ray is sure to satisfy.

*   *   *

The Dewey Decimal System of Love by Josephine Carr
New York: New American Library, 2003
Humorous Fiction, Romance, Women's Fiction, Mystery

Something happens when a woman hits forty and has never been married. It starts to feel like a permanent condition. Certain clues? Her friends might stop fixing her up, or her therapist may start to talk about the value of solitude. The biggest indication, though, is when flannel nightgowns and soft comforters start to look downright sexy at the end of the day.

Forty-year-old Allison Sheffield, reference librarian and spinster, is just starting to give up on men altogether when she goes to the symphony one night and falls in love at first sight with Aleksi Kullio, the conductor of the Philadelphia Philharmonic. She knows it's ridiculous to fall for this man—not only is he married, he is a very important person and there would be no chance at all to meet him. Then Allison gets a brilliant idea. She sends the conductor an e-mail notice about a new Stravinsky biography, just as a library public service announcement, and he actually answers! Oh joy! Allison is in love! But there's that darn wife of his, who has started coming into the library to do research on a murder mystery she's writing. Wait a minute, Allison thinks. A murder mystery? What is she up to?

Discover how Allison tries to use the Dewey decimal system to solve all her problems in this lighthearted look at a modern librarian's love life in *The Dewey Decimal System of Love* by Josephine Carr.

*   *   *

Isn't It Romantic? by Ron Hansen
New York: HarperCollins, 2003
Humorous Fiction

Natalie and Pierre are from France; they're young, engaged, and fighting. Natalie, a librarian, resents that Pierre flirts with every woman he sees and sleeps with every woman he can. Pierre, the son of a famous vintner, resents that Natalie expects him to be monogamous. After all, he tells her daily, he's French!

Natalie decides to escape on a bus tour of America. Pierre follows her and joins the tour despite her strong objections. When the bus breaks down, they end up stranded in Seldom, Nebraska, population 395. The townspeople are thrilled to have real French people in their midst and volunteer to help. Natalie ends up in the "women-only" boarding house run by a retired French teacher who can't speak French. Pierre is taken in by Owen, owner of the local gas station/video store, who hates cars and dreams of becoming an international winemaker.

Natalie and Pierre each begin trysts with locals in an attempt to make the other jealous. When the good folks of Seldom get involved in wedding plans and showers, mistaken identities and hilarious misunderstandings abound.

Isn't It Romantic? a screwball comedy by Ron Hansen.

*   *   *

Her by Laura Zigman
New York: Knopf, 2002
Humorous Fiction, Romance

Okay, let me just say that I used to be normal. I used to have dreams, goals . . . you know, a life. How did everything go so wrong? How did I lose control? I still haven't figured it all out yet but I do know one thing: It's all because of her!

Let me start at the beginning. My name is Elise, I've recently moved from New York to Washington, D.C., and I'm engaged to be married.

I'm not going to tell you that my life was perfect. There were times when I questioned giving up my career at Sassy to move to D.C. and go back to school. I do feel a little overwhelmed when trying to plan the perfect wedding, and my fiancé, Donald, has a few quirks. Well . . . two, really. First, he is obsessed with his weight. Second, he has a tendency to pull his pants down when he's upset. Yes, you heard right. I'm not quite sure how this started or why he does it, but it does cause problems when he does it in public.

So, okay, things weren't perfect but now they're a mess and it's all her fault! Who is she? you ask. She is Adrienne. Rich, successful, and beautiful. Adrienne is tall, willowy, and big chested. She's Yale educated, French, perfect, moving to D.C.—and she's Donald's ex-fiancée. It's true. My Donald, the love of my life, used to be engaged to . . .

Her, a modern romantic comedy by Laura Zigman.

* * *

The Rich Part of Life by Jim Kokoris
New York: St. Martin's, 2001
Humorous Fiction

When Teddy Pappas's father won a giant lottery jackpot by playing the same numbers his dead wife always played, Teddy thought the rich part of their lives was about to begin. After all, they won an indecent amount of money and had their names and pictures in the papers, and strangers sent them letters filled with sad requests for money. But instead of buying fancy new cars or moving to a larger house, Teddy's father insisted that Teddy and his brother keep their same routines. Oh sure, Aunt Bess moved in to help take care of them, and Uncle Frank, a producer of cheesy Hollywood movies, suddenly appeared, but for the most part, life continued on in the same drab way, to Teddy's disappointment. Just as Teddy starts constructing elaborate lies to tell at school about the wonderful things his father is buying, danger appears in the form of a mysterious stranger who shows up in a truck with Tennessee license plates, following Teddy home from school. Who is this man, and what does he want with Teddy? To keep the boys safe, Teddy's father hires Maurice, a bodyguard, who moves in along with Sylvanius, a former soap opera vampire star. Just when dinner conversation starts to get interesting, Teddy becomes worried about Mrs. Wilcott, a gold-digging divorcée who has designs on Teddy's dad. Can life get any more confusing? Join the Pappas family as they negotiate life's twists and turns as reluctant millionaires in *The Rich Part of Life* by Jim Kokoris.

MULTICULTURAL FICTION

Definition: Multicultural novels focus on or explore a race, religion, or culture different from the readers'. For example, if you are a Chinese person living in China, a book about Chinese people living in China is not multicultural. The same title, however, would be an example of multicultural fiction to an American. The same is true for people of various races or religions living in the same country, for example, a book focusing on a Hispanic community in California would be an example of multicultural fiction for an African American reader who lives in California. Multicultural fiction can be set in any time or place and is often found in other genres.

Purpose: Enable readers to explore or gain insight into a race, religion, or culture different from their own.

General Appeal Characteristics

Enables readers to visit a foreign country, explore a particular culture, or gain insight or understanding of an unfamiliar religion.

Setting is a crucial element in this genre. Details and descriptions must paint a vivid picture so that readers can visualize, or even place themselves within, the story.

Language is used to draw readers in and to create realistic, well-rounded characters. Often dialects or foreign words or phrases are used to enhance readers' feeling of visiting a foreign place or interacting with an unfamiliar culture or religion. Consistency is key here: If a character uses a certain dialect or style of speech, he or she must use it throughout the story or the character and the novel lose credibility.

Multicultural fiction is usually character rather than event or action driven. This means that it is the people of the race, religion, or culture explored that are the most important element of the story. Although major events often take place, it is the manner in which a specific group of characters react to or deal with the event that is important, not the event itself. Characters are well developed and believable and must be consistent with the culture they represent.

Samples

Cry, the Beloved Country by Alan Paton
New York: Scribner, 1951
Multicultural Fiction, Historical Fiction

Stephen Kumalo is a Zulu pastor in a small mountain town in South Africa. He has a good life, a house, enough food to eat, and a good wife. He is well liked and respected, a leader in his village. Yes, life is good—until the letter comes.

The letter is from Johannesburg and tells him to come quickly. His sister Gertrude is very ill. Stephen doesn't want to go; he is afraid of Johannesburg. The city seems to swallow people up, and Stephen dreads the long and dangerous trip.

But this journey will prove to be more perilous than he could have imagined. Stephen knows there are changes occurring in his country, that some of the whites in charge want to dictate where blacks can and cannot live. What he doesn't know is how strong the feelings of hate and fear have become. He isn't aware of the assault his dignity is about to undergo, but he will soon.

Stephen Kumalo is a black man traveling to Johannesburg, South Africa, at a time when apartheid is just beginning—and his life, his family, and his homeland will never be the same in *Cry, the Beloved Country* by Alan Paton.

*   *   *

Balzac and the Little Chinese Seamstress by Dai Sijie
New York: Knopf, 2001
Multicultural Fiction, Historical Fiction

It seemed like a prison sentence. Two young men, seventeen and eighteen years old, are sent to a remote mountain village and given jobs carrying pails of excrement up and down a hill. They cannot continue their schooling, they cannot have any contact with their friends and family, and they are forced to do whatever the local village leader commands them to do. What horrible crime did they commit to be banished to the mountains for four years? Nothing. As part of Chairman Mao's Cultural Revolution, their parents were designated "class enemies," and therefore the sons had to be "reeducated" before they could rejoin civilization.

The two young men are clever and resourceful, however, and the local people discover they have a talent for storytelling. The village leader gives them a day off from their labors each week in order to travel to the nearest town to see a movie and retell it to the villagers when they return. This helps relieve the tedium of their existence—as does the discovery of a hidden treasure. Another city boy has been hiding a whole suitcase of forbidden Western novels, so the two boys plot to steal it, knowing that the other boy cannot reveal the secret. Now, in addition to their weekly movies, they dare to retell the story of the *Count of Monte Cristo* to the local tailor and to read Balzac to his beautiful daughter, the seamstress.

Who knew that Balzac could have such a romantic effect on the seamstress? When one of the boys falls in love with her, they discover that literature does indeed have the power to save—or doom—one's soul. *Balzac and the Little Chinese Seamstress* by Dai Sijie.

*   *   *

Memoirs of a Geisha by Arthur Golden
New York: Knopf, 1997
Multicultural Fiction, Women's Fiction, Historical Fiction

Chiyo was born to a poor fisherman in a small Japanese village. Times were hard for her family and she often spent her days dreaming of a better life. Her favorite fantasy was that Mr. Tanaka, the richest man in the village, would adopt her and take her to live in his grand house.

Chiyo is thrilled, sure that her dreams have come true, when her father tells her that Mr. Tanaka wants to see her. Imagine her devastation when she learns that Mr. Tanaka has purchased Chiyo from her father and sold her to a geisha house in Kyoto.

Chiyo now belongs to Auntie, the harsh woman who runs the house. She is a slave, at the beck and call of all the geishas, and must do whatever she is told without complaint. The only way out is to repay the money that Auntie paid for her, but she soon learns that this is an impossible task. Every day her debt grows as she is charged for the food she eats, the clothes she wears, and the lessons on how to be a geisha she is forced to endure.

The lessons seem endless. She must learn to sing, play several instruments, and dance. She must learn how to walk gracefully and sit for hours in a kimono. She must master the fine art of conversation and learn how to please a man so that he will pay large sums of money just to spend time with her.

Here is a spellbinding tale that takes you into the mythical world of the geisha in 1930s Japan. Uncover the secret ceremonies and discover what daily life was like in Arthur Golden's *Memoirs of a Geisha*.

*   *   *

Moloka'i by Alan Brennert
New York: St. Martin's, 2003
Multicultural Fiction, Historical Fiction

Life is idyllic for seven-year-old Rachel Kalama on the island of Oahu in the late 1890s. Her days are spent helping her mother make poi for the family, going to school barefoot, and playing with her sister and two brothers. One day, however, her mother discovers a bleeding gash on her leg that Rachel didn't even know was there. Her mother tries everything to heal the spot on Rachel's leg. She visits a *kahuna*, or local medicine man, for special medicine. The family has a *ho'oponopono*, or ceremony, to heal things between family members. They go to church and pray for a miracle. But none of these things work, and Rachel is forced to wear long dresses and shoes to school so that no one can see the spots that are spreading on her body.

When Rachel cannot hide her disease anymore, she is arrested as a leper and sent to a hospital to be examined. She hates it there; the deformed patients frighten her and she misses her family. Then the most horrible thing of all happens—she is exiled to Kalaupapa, the leper colony on the island of Moloka'i. How will she live without her mama, her papa, and her brothers and sister? How can she be taken away from her home and all that she loves? She is only seven years old and feels as if her heart is going to break.

Based on a true story, *Moloka'i* by Alan Brennert is a fictionalized account of one girl's struggle for a meaningful existence amidst loneliness, despair, and a hopeless future. With courage and determination, Rachel learns that she can still live a full and happy life, despite the obstacles that she faces along the way.

*   *   *

Sister of My Heart by Chitra Banerjee Divakaruni
New York: Doubleday, 1999
Multicultural Fiction, Women's Fiction
   Sister of My Heart is a story of duality. Set in the two worlds of India and America, it is a contemporary story steeped in the traditions and superstitions of long-ago India. It is the story of two families forged together through tragedy and ripped apart by deception. It is the story of Anju and Sudha.
   Anju: brilliant, defiant yet plain. The privileged daughter of an upper-caste Calcutta family, Anju casts off her family's expectations and defies traditions when she marries an American and moves to California.
   Sudha: beautiful, tenderhearted, obedient. Daughter of the family black sheep, Sudha is as quiet as Anju is loud. Determined to make up for her parents' numerous shortcomings, Sudha suppresses her own dreams and surrenders herself to a wretched life in an arranged marriage.
   Anju and Sudha . . . born on the same day, raised in the same house, loved and taught by the same women—cousins by blood but sisters of the heart. *Sister of My Heart* by Chitra Banerjee Divakaruni.

*   *   *

An Almost Perfect Moment by Binnie Kirshenbaum
New York: Ecco, 2004
Multicultural Fiction, Humor
   Everyone agrees that Valentine Kessler has a face like an angel. She is beautiful. And it isn't just her beauty that strikes you. She looks as if she knows everything in the universe, as if she knows all your secrets, including the ones you don't dare admit even to yourself. And if this isn't enough, Valentine has something else unique about her—she is the spitting image of the Blessed Virgin Mary as she appeared to Bernadette at Lourdes. The problem? Valentine is a good Jewish girl, and her mother is very concerned about her behavior.
   You see, Valentine is fascinated with the Catholic Church. She hums "Ave Maria" when she thinks no one is listening, she reads about the lives of the saints, and she has a raging crush on her geometry teacher, Mr. Wosileski. Her mother, Miriam, has lectured her about Jewish last names, and Wosileski is definitely not a Jewish name, but this does not stop Valentine from visiting him one evening. Perhaps she somehow knew that her showing up in his

dismal bachelor apartment was his fantasy come to life—but alas! Life does not always live up to our fantasies. After their brief encounter, Mr. Wosileski becomes even lonelier and more disillusioned about his life, but this is typical of encounters with Valentine. Somehow, just her presence shatters the hopes and dreams of everyone around her.

What is a miracle, after all? Is Valentine a foolish teenager who gets terribly confused, or one of the chosen few who inspires devotion and faith? Either way, this book will make you think about faith and miracles and the power of the imagination. Certainly, the people around Valentine find their own beliefs turned upside down in this darkly comic and richly ironic novel. *An Almost Perfect Moment* by Binnie Kirshenbaum.

* * *

My Year of Meats by Ruth L. Ozeki
New York: Viking, 1998
Multicultural Fiction, Women's Fiction

Akiko Ueno is a young Japanese housewife who lives with her ad agency executive husband in Tokyo. Akiko has a secret: She is deliberately sabotaging her husband's plans for a family by refusing to gain weight. She is so thin that her bones ache and having a baby is out of the question.

It's not that she doesn't want children. She would love to have a baby of her own; the problem is her husband. When they were dating, Joichi was warm, loving, and supportive. Now that they're married he's become a dominating, arrogant, patronizing sleazeball who loves all things American and demands that she call him John. Akiko can't wait until he makes another one of his business trips to America so she can have some peace.

Jane Takagi-Little is a documentary filmmaker who lives in New York City and is desperate for a job. When her phone rings at 2:00 a.m. the last thing she expects is a job offer, but that's exactly what she gets. And not just any job: she will be the coordinator of the production team for a new half-hour Japanese television show called *My American Wife!*

Jane is thrilled until she meets her boss. The company's representative is from Japan and makes trips to America to oversee the filming of the series. Joichi (John) Ueno is a dominating, arrogant, patronizing sleazeball! Jane can't wait until he goes back to Tokyo so she can have some peace.

Told alternately by these two vastly different women, *My Year of Meats* by Ruth L. Ozeki gives a touching, hilarious look at each culture and the impact that a television series—and a sleazeball—can have on both sides of the world.

* * *

The Kite Runner by Khaled Hosseini
New York: Riverhead, 2003
Multicultural Fiction

Amir and Hassan were as close as two boys could be without being related. They did everything together from the time they got up in the morning until they went to bed at night. There was just one thing that separated them: school. Amir attended school because he was the son of a wealthy man. Hassan, the son of Amir's father's servant, was not allowed to go to school. He was also a Hazara, a member of the shunned ethnic minority, and forbidden to read or write.

Amir loved Hassan like a brother, but one day a terrible thing happened. He witnessed some boys assaulting Hassan just because he was a Hazara, and he did nothing to stop it. Then he treated Hassan very badly afterward because of his intense guilt over the incident. This caused such a problem in the household that Hassan and his father decided to leave, and the two boys lost touch forever.

Many years later, after Amir and his father immigrated to the United States to escape the war in Afghanistan, Amir receives a phone call from an old family friend, who tells him he's dying. He wants Amir to come back to Afghanistan, a dying man's wish. Despite the risk and danger of returning to Kabul, Amir knows that he must try to find Hassan again. "Come," says the old man to Amir. "There is a way to be good again." He can only hope it's not too late for two lost friends to find each other once again. *The Kite Runner* by Khaled Hosseini.

MYSTERY

Definition: Mysteries contain a puzzle, in the form of a crime, which needs to be solved. They can be set in any time period or location, real or imagined. There are numerous subgenres to mysteries, including police procedurals, murder mysteries, culinary mysteries, private detectives, amateur sleuths, mysteries that feature animals, humorous mysteries, historical mysteries, and others. Series often play an important role in this genre.

Purpose: Challenge the reader to correctly solve the puzzle presented with the clues provided along with or before the main character.

General Appeal Characteristics

Mysteries follow a comfortable pattern: a crime is committed; a person or group investigates the crime, following clues and interviewing suspects; the crime is solved; and the perpetrator is brought to justice. This basic pattern enables readers to enjoy a level of comfort and security and frees them to boldly explore the many twists, turns, and dangers associated with the genre.

All characters, including secondary characters, whether investigators, suspects, or witnesses, play an important part in the story. Backstory is interspersed in the novel to give some characters depth, while others are left elusive and unknown.

Clues are given throughout the story in a manner that requires careful attention to detail. Recognizing and following these clues will enable readers to solve the mystery.

The setting of the novel is extremely important and often becomes a character itself. Having a realistic and consistent setting is often a crucial element in the book's appeal.

Pacing—or, to be more exact, a particular pacing—is not an issue in this genre. Many mysteries are fast-paced, with witty dialogue, multiple crimes, or graphic details. Others are slow, leisurely investigations that allow readers to settle in to the time period or location.

Mysteries often provide readers with a series of books to enjoy. Many readers become attached to a particular character or setting, and a series allows them to follow a particular character or continue to experience a certain time or location.

A good ending is a crucial element to this genre. At the end of a mystery the crime should be solved and the perpetrator (if still alive) should be brought to justice. The puzzle *must* be able to be solved using the clues provided within the story. Nothing irritates fans of this genre more that having a solution "come out of left field." By this we mean that the clues needed to solve the crime were not provided within the novel or that the perpetrator is a new or unknown character. Readers must be given a fair chance to solve the crime along with the investigator.

Samples

Trace Evidence by Elizabeth Becka
New York: Hyperion, 2005
Mystery, Women's Fiction

Destiny Pierson knew she was in trouble the moment she woke up. Not the "your room is a mess" or "you were late" kind of trouble, but big trouble. The beautiful sixteen-year-old looked around the gray brick room wondering where she was and how she got here. She felt strange; she was groggy, nauseous, and unable to move.

The last thing she remembered was going to a party with some of her friends. Was this their idea of a joke? Were some of the kids from school, jealous of her popularity, wealth, and good grades, playing some kind of mean trick on her?

As Destiny's head cleared she realized that this was not just some joke or prank. She was chained to a chair and her feet were stuck in a bucket of cement. As panic rose, Destiny heard him come up from behind her. "Who are you?" she screamed. "Let me go! Do you know who I am? I'm the mayor's daughter!"

Destiny's body was found the next day; the second such murder in two days. Evelyn James has been a forensic scientist with the Cleveland Medical Examiner's Trace Evidence Department for more than ten years and in that time she's seen thousands of murders, but she's never seen anything like this.

Who is killing these girls, and why pick such a cruel, bizarre method? Now that the mayor's daughter is a victim, the case has become a media circus, and Evelyn and her team are under even more pressure to solve the case and arrest the killer . . . and do it fast.

Elizabeth Becka, herself a veteran forensic scientist, uses her own experience to craft a riveting page-turner in her debut novel *Trace Evidence*.

*　　*　　*

The Defense by D. W. Buffa
New York: Henry Holt, 1997
Mystery

Defense attorney Joseph Antonelli never lost a case. Never. Somehow Mr. Antonelli possessed a special gift that allowed him to persuade jury after jury that his client was innocent—even when the evidence clearly showed otherwise. He never worried about justice or conscience or morality—he was paid to do a job, and he did it well.

As the years passed, Mr. Antonelli earned a great deal of money and an excellent reputation. Then one day a judge asked him to take on a case that he was certain to lose. The accused was a convicted drug dealer charged with raping his twelve-year-old stepdaughter. Despite his personal distaste for the man, Mr. Antonelli had no problem defending a client he knew was guilty. The problem? In this case the verdict led to a murder, and it looked like the defense was to blame. Suddenly Mr. Antonelli began to have doubts about his own role in the justice system, wondering how he could have ever helped a guilty man go free. *The Defense* by D. W. Buffa.

*　　*　　*

A Dangerous Road by Kris Nelscott
New York: St. Martin's Minotaur, 2000
Mystery, Historical Fiction, Multicultural Fiction

The year is 1968, and racial tensions are running high in Memphis, the home of private investigator Smokey Dalton. Demonstrations turn violent and the streets are not safe. Smokey's old friend Martin Luther King Jr. is planning to visit the city, and Smokey has been enlisted to help keep the order, a job he is not relishing.

In the middle of the chaos, a young white woman appears, asking why Smokey would be the recipient of a sizable chunk of money from her mother's estate. Since this is a mystery Smokey himself would like to solve, he agrees to take the case after warning her that he may uncover some unpleasant secrets.

As violence and destruction take over the city, Smokey finds himself drawn deeper and deeper into a web of fear and deception, so much so that he no longer can trust his own beloved city or the past he thought he knew. It's a dangerous road he's started down; he can only hope that it won't turn out to be a dead end. *A Dangerous Road* by Kris Nelscott.

✻   ✻   ✻

Hearts and Bones by Margaret Lawrence
New York: Avon, 1996
Mystery, Historical Fiction, Women's Fiction

In the late 1700s the residents of Rufford, Maine, are wondering what else could go wrong. It seems as though the town itself is cursed. First, there are all the people who were wounded or driven insane by the Revolutionary War. Then there's poor Hannah Trevor, the local midwife, whose first three children died of diphtheria, whose husband ran off and left her, and whose last child was born both deaf and mute. And now, in the middle of a brutal winter, Anthea Emory, a young wife and mother, has been found raped and murdered in her home!

It was Hannah who found the body of the poor woman and, nearby, a letter signed by Anthea, naming her murderers, one of whom is Daniel Josselyn.

Daniel is a wealthy, upstanding citizen of Rufford, and Hannah can't believe he is capable of this evil. Nor can she understand why the criminals would leave such an incriminating piece of evidence behind. The letter was in plain sight, and Hannah knows that Daniel can read. It just doesn't make any sense until Hannah discovers that Anthea *couldn't* read or write. Now she knows that the letter is a fake, meant to mislead the town and implicate the wrong people.

So who did write the letter and who is the fiend roaming the streets of Rufford? As more residents are found murdered, Hannah decides to solve the crimes herself in *Hearts and Bones*, the first in the Hannah Trevor Mystery Series by Margaret Lawrence.

✻   ✻   ✻

The Serpent in the Garden by Janet Gleeson
New York: Simon & Schuster, 2005
Mystery, Historical Fiction

The serpentine necklace was exquisite. It consisted of a dozen emeralds set in gold links, and it was shaped like a snake with the tail and head joined at the neck. Little did the famous artist Joshua Pope know that some people would do anything to get their hands on that necklace—even commit murder.

It's the summer of 1765, and Joshua Pope has been commissioned to do a wedding portrait of Herbert Bentnick and his fiancée, Sabine. Joshua has barely begun painting when Sabine discovers a dead body in the greenhouse. Then Sabine's emerald necklace turns up missing, and Joshua is the chief suspect. He starts an investigation in order to save his reputation, and he discovers that nearly everyone in the household has a secret to hide.

Why was this necklace so special that someone would commit murder for it? Joshua Pope is so close to the answer he can feel the killer's breath on the back of his neck—and he has good reason to be nervous. There is a serpent in the garden, just waiting for the right opportunity to shut Joshua up forever. *The Serpent in the Garden* by Janet Gleeson.

*   *   *

Blood Ties by Lori G. Armstrong
Palm Beach, FL: Medallion, 2005
Mystery, Multicultural Fiction

Life in a small town can be hard, especially when you're a girl with a reputation. Julie Collins has been known for her fast-talking, hard-drinking, chain-smoking ways ever since high school. Now that she's in her thirties, she knows she should stop the self-destructive behavior and just grow up. The trouble is, she's never recovered from the violent death of her Lakota half-brother, Ben, whose unsolved murder haunts her dreams at night.

When an old classmate's daughter turns up dead in a case very similar to her brother's, Julie jumps at the chance to get involved. Her friend Kevin is a private investigator, and the two start asking questions around town. They discover that the dead girl's mother was raped and the girl had recently discovered her real father's identity. It soon becomes clear that Julie and Kevin have stumbled onto one of this town's biggest secrets—and that someone will do anything, even murder, to stop them in their tracks. *Blood Ties* by Lori G. Armstrong.

*   *   *

Bait by C. J. Songer
New York: Scribner, 1998
Mystery

Meg Gillis didn't like working on Saturdays but realized it was necessary sometimes, especially when you're trying to build a new business. Meg and her partner, Mike Johnson, are ex-cops who have started a security business outside Beverly Hills.

Mike is the one who gets most of their business. He still has contacts with the police and people just feel more comfortable talking with a man about security. Meg is usually stuck in the office doing the paperwork, paying the bills, and making sure the new systems are installed and working correctly, but today, Mike promised he'd be here to help, so where was he?

When the phone rings on Mike's private line, Meg is sure it's him, making some lame excuse for not coming in, for leaving her to do all the paperwork alone, again. But when she answers the phone she finds herself talking to a hysterical man with a heavy accent, who tells her his son has been kidnapped and that she must bring Mike . . . now!

Unable to find Mike, Meg decides to take the call herself. After calling the police she heads out to the Beverly Hills address. Upon arrival she's greeted by Sergeant Joe Reilly of the police Special Tactics Unit and a very calm man claiming, in perfect English, that he has no idea what's going on; he never made a phone call and he doesn't have a son.

Meg now finds herself under suspicion of harassment and while she's being questioned at the police station, her car is stolen, only to be recovered the next day in another city, filled with blood.

Is Meg paranoid or is she being set up? Who is this Sergeant Reilly, and what is he really after? Whose blood is in her car? And, most important, where's Mike?

Bait, a taut, compelling mystery that will leave you guessing to the end by C. J. Songer.

*   *   *

Death al Dente by Peter King
New York: St. Martin's, 1999
Mystery

Actor/restaurateur Desmond Lansdowne is on a mission to open the absolutely, unquestionably best Italian restaurant in London. This will be the jewel in his crown, his legacy. He's got the money, he's got the name recognition, and he's got the clout. There's just one problem: He doesn't have a chef.

To solve this little problem, he hires the Gourmet Detective and sends him to Italy to decide which of the country's top three chefs should be hired for the new London restaurant.

The mission is supposed to be top secret. Everyone's supposed to believe the Gourmet Detective is writing a travel food and wine guide. But when people start turning up dead and a mysterious man dressed as a monk threatens his life, the Gourmet Detective knows the gig's up. Who told about his true reason for being in Italy? Are these famed chefs really willing to kill for this job? And why do the police think he's a suspect? Finding a new chef is the least of his problems; now he has to clear his name, solve the murders and try to get out of Italy alive.

With a winning recipe of murder, fun wine facts, and mouth-watering descriptions of Italian cuisine, *Death al Dente* by Peter King will delight any culinary mystery fan.

NONFICTION

Definition: A book that instructs or provides true or factual information on a real subject or that provides insight into a culture or society such as a fairy tale, legend, or tall tale, or a work of literature such as a play, poem, or short story.

Purpose: Provide the reader with instruction or factual information or insight on a real subject or to provoke thoughts or feelings through the use of literature.

General Appeal Characteristics

The material contained in nonfiction books is factual and provides the reader with new or needed information. Readers turn to nonfiction titles to keep informed on subjects that interest them or to answer questions that have arisen in their lives.

Many readers feel that nonfiction allows them to expand their scope of knowledge and better themselves; they often feel that reading fiction is a waste of time.

Enables readers to learn a new skill or understand a new concept, culture, time, or place.

Samples

Inside the Kingdom: My Life in Saudi Arabia by Carmen Bin Ladin
New York: Warner, 2004
Nonfiction

On September 11, 2001, Carmen bin Ladin and her three daughters, living in Geneva, Switzerland, watched in horror as the two towers of the World Trade Center fell. Like millions of others around the world, they were devastated by the terrible acts of murder and destruction in the United States, a country that they loved, a country they considered to be their second home. They spent the day glued to their television, awaiting any information that might help to answer their questions and alleviate their fears.

Unlike others, Carmen knew who was behind this vicious act of terrorism. She had met him and knew firsthand of his hatred for America and the freedoms that it stood for. Long before CNN started saying the name, she knew that the man responsible was her brother-in-law, Osama Bin Laden.

In 1973 Carmen Dufour met Yeslam Bin Laden. He was the tenth son of a wealthy, powerful Saudi Arabian family spending the summer in Geneva. Yeslam was everything Carmen had dreamed of in a boyfriend; he was attentive, charming, and sociable. He treated her as an equal, loved her spirit, and shared her dreams of making a new life in the United States.

In 1974 they were married. The wedding took place in Saudi Arabia. It was Carmen's first visit to the country and the first look she had of the restrictions placed on the women who lived there. She was stunned, but not worried. Yeslam wasn't like that—and besides, they were going to live in America.

In 1976 Carmen and Yeslam moved into the family compound in Saudi Arabia and her life was forever changed. Never could she have imagined living this way. She was cut off from all she knew and loved, her husband now treated her more like a pet than a partner, and his family considered her to be an alien who forced her way into their lives.

In *Inside the Kingdom: My Life in Saudi Arabia*, Carmen Bin Ladin tells of her life inside one of the most restrictive and fundamentalist Islamic countries in the world. You will read of her daily struggles for even the most basic human rights; of her haunting encounters with her husband's hate-filled, fanatical younger brother Osama; and of her desperate fourteen-year battle to end the hold this family had on her life and the lives of her daughters.

✳ ✳ ✳

Fat Girl: A True Story by Judith Moore
New York: Hudson Street Press, 2005
Nonfiction

Judith Moore has been fat almost all of her life. Although she didn't start out being fat (really, who does?), it didn't take long before a sad and dysfunctional family life caused her to overeat and become a fat little girl. Life was not easy for young Judith Moore. She had to endure name-calling and a lack of friends. She had to undergo painful beatings when her mother's diets failed to bring her weight down. And worst of all, she had to bear the pain of a lonely childhood when she realized that no one really loved her.

This heart-wrenching story does not mince words or sugarcoat the truth. The truth is, we are not nice to fat children, nor do we understand or appreciate them. We tease them when they are young, and we judge them when we see them in line at McDonald's. But no matter how mean or judgmental we are to fat people, they are a hundred times more so to themselves. Even if you've never struggled with your weight, you will easily identify with the hurt, shame, and betrayal portrayed in *Fat Girl: A True Story*.

✳ ✳ ✳

Sunk without a Sound: The Tragic Colorado River Honeymoon of Glen and Bessie Hyde by Brad Dimock
Flagstaff, AZ: Fretwater, 2001

Nonfiction

On October 28, 1928, Glen and Bessie Hyde set off in a homemade boat to run the Green and Colorado rivers from Green River, Utah, to Needles, California. The trip would be more than eight hundred miles long and take them through the beautiful but treacherous Grand Canyon of Arizona, home of some of the most dangerous white water in the world.

Although Bessie had never been on a river, Glen was an experienced boatman who had traversed the rapids of the Salmon River with few problems. The two had been planning this trip since their wedding seven months before. They had studied every book on and map of the Grand Canyon they could find and had read all the information on every previous expedition.

Bessie, who would be the first woman to make the trip, was a writer and would keep a diary of their experience. They planned on writing a book detailing their journey and then going on a lecture circuit to inform and entertain people with their tales. It would be the adventure of a lifetime.

Glen and Bessie Hyde disappeared on November 30, 1928, roughly halfway through their journey. Although several extensive searches were performed, no trace was ever found of the couple.

Sixty-eight years later, Brad Dimock and his wife, Jeri Ledbetter, decided to build their own boat and repeat the Hydes' journey from their last known sighting at Phantom Ranch to the place where they disappeared forever. Using historical documents, interviews with people who participated in the search, family papers, and parts of the diary that Bessie kept of the journey, Dimock sorts through the truth, myth, and legend to try to answer the question: What happened to Glen and Bessie Hyde? *Sunk without a Sound: The Tragic Colorado River Honeymoon of Glen and Bessie Hyde* by Brad Dimock.

❊   ❊   ❊

A Million Little Pieces by James Frey
New York: Doubleday, 2003
Nonfiction

Imagine that you wake up in an airplane. You have no idea where you came from, how you got onto this airplane, or where you are going. In fact, you have no memory at all of anything that has happened in the last two weeks.

Imagine that when you wake up in this airplane, your four front teeth are gone, your eyes are swollen almost shut, your nose is broken, and your cheek has a huge gash in it. You feel dizzy and sick. You check your pockets and discover that you are missing your wallet, your money, and your identification. Your clothes are covered in a combination of vomit, urine, saliva, and blood.

If this had happened to you or me, we would think we had been beaten and kidnapped. When this happened to James Frey, however, he knew that it was because of drugs and alcohol. He knew that his addictions had finally gotten so bad that he had blacked out for more than two weeks, was probably involved with criminals or worse, and was now flying home to Chicago so that his parents could get him the help he needed to get off drugs and alcohol once and for all.

This is the story of a young man who was ready to give up on himself but somehow found the strength, courage, and faith to overcome his addictions. Despite the controversy surrounding the truthfulness of his book, Frey's firsthand account offers a revealing and compelling look at one addict's attempt to reconstruct his life in order to save it. *A Million Little Pieces* by James Frey.

* * *

In the Heart of the Sea: The Tragedy of the Whaleship Essex by Nathaniel Philbrick
New York: Viking, 2000
Nonfiction
Have you ever wondered just how far you would go to survive? I remember hearing about the man who was caught when a boulder shifted and pinned his arm while he was rock climbing in Utah. Trapped, alone, and facing certain death from thirst and starvation, he cut off his own arm with a penknife and walked to safety. I wonder: could I do that? Could I walk hundreds of miles or tread water for days? Could I kill someone to survive?

In February 1821 the crew of the whale ship *Dauphin* came across a whaleboat floating off the coast of Chile. The first thing that struck them as they looked into the tiny vessel was that it was littered with bones. Next, they saw men huddled in the boat sucking the marrow from some of these bones. The bones had been gnawed on until they were splintered and stripped of all meat. The bones were clutched tightly in the desperate men's hands. The bones were human.

One of the most riveting sea disasters of all time was the sinking of the whale ship *Essex* in 1820. Herman Melville used this event to write the end of *Moby-Dick*, and children of the nineteenth century read and studied about the *Essex* the way today's children read about the *Titanic*.

Twenty men escaped the ship in whaleboats after an enraged whale sank it. Only eight survived the desperate voyage to the South American coast. What happened during those months at sea?

With fascinating details on whaling and Nantucket, and using survivor interviews and a newly found journal written by the cabin boy aboard the *Essex*, Nathaniel Philbrick brings to life this amazing story: *In the Heart of the Sea: The Tragedy of the Whaleship Essex*.

* * *

A Round-Heeled Woman: My Late-Life Adventures in Sex and Romance by
  Jane Juska
New York: Villard, 2003
Nonfiction
  Jane Juska was sixty-six, divorced, and celibate. One day she was reflecting
upon her life and what the future held. Although she had made a conscious
decision to be single, she realized she was not happy living that way. As she
contemplated the idea of never having sex again, she decided to take action.
She composed an ad and placed it in a national newspaper. The ad read:
"Before I turn 67—next March—I would like to have a lot of sex with a man
I like. If you want to talk first, Trollope works fine for me."
  "Round-heeled woman" is an old-fashioned term for a woman who is
promiscuous. Even though some people might consider Jane to be easy, she
doesn't end up having as much sex with as many different men as you might
think. As her ad stated, her goal was not to have sex with a lot of different
men; her goal was to find one man she liked. Some of the men she meets are
as lonely as she is, some are crass and opportunistic, and some are not so
nice to her. In fact, some of her encounters make her feel uncomfortable and
depressed—so much so that she almost gives the whole thing up. Honest and
direct, Jane's account of her sexual adventures may fascinate some people
and shock the rest, but everyone will agree that her approach certainly was
unique! *A Round-Heeled Woman: My Late-Life Adventures in Sex and
Romance* by Jane Juska.

*   *   *

Honor Lost: Love and Death in Modern-Day Jordan by Norma Khouri
New York: Atria, 2003
Nonfiction
  The women of Jordan have come a long way; at least that's what the men
of Jordan want you to believe. After all, they'll tell you, women can now
vote, go to college, and have jobs. This is all true, as far as it goes.
  It is true that since 1989, women in Jordan can vote—as long as the men
in their family give them permission and they vote as the men tell them to.
They can go to college—as long as they have permission and take the classes
the men in their family tell them to. They can have jobs—as long as they
work where and when they're told, don't fall behind in their housework, and
immediately turn over 100 percent of their pay to the men in their family.
  There's also another, uglier reality that the women of Jordan must live
with every day . . . death. As in many other Middle Eastern countries,
women in Jordan can be murdered in broad daylight, with many witnesses,
and the police will never investigate their death. Their killer will never be
sent to jail; in fact, he will be lauded for his actions and held up as a role

model for other men in the community. The killer will be one of the men in the family and their murder will be called an "honor killing."

Honor Lost: Love and Death in Modern-Day Jordan by Norma Khouri is the true story of one of these killings. Dalia was murdered by her father because he suspected her of being a whore. He stabbed her in the chest fourteen times, then waited until he knew she couldn't be saved before he called the ambulance to take her body away. The autopsy showed that Dalia was a virgin. The police never questioned her father; he never showed any signs of regret or remorse; his actions were considered honorable.

The women of Jordan have come a long way; at least that's what the men of Jordan want you to believe.

*   *   *

Tender at the Bone: Growing Up at the Table by Ruth Reichl
New York: Random House, 1998
Nonfiction

Everyone has childhood memories of food. Most of the time, these are fond memories of Mom's meatloaf or Dad's blueberry pancakes. For Ruth Reichl, former restaurant critic at the *New York Times*, her memories center on her mother's creative use of leftovers, which she used for soups, stews, and party fare. Yes, Ruth's mother, otherwise known as the Queen of Mold, thought nothing of using old sour cream for St. Patrick's Day (after all, it was already green), old crabmeat for soup (extra sherry covered up the smell), and apple pie in her "Everything Stew." Once she even woke up Ruth's dad just to have him taste something and after he spat it out in the sink, she smiled and exclaimed, "Just as I thought. Spoiled!"

At a very young age, Ruth discovered that food was a way of making sense of the world. As she grew older, she met many people who introduced her to the wonder of gastronomical delights, like Mrs. Peavy, the famed Baltimore socialite who taught her how to make a proper Beef Wellington, and Monsieur du Crois, who gave her her first taste of a soufflé. Interspersed with the recipes that contributed to her coming of age, food-wise, this memoir is chock-full of rich characters and tasty treats. So sit down, grab a cup of tea and an Artpark Brownie (recipe on page 244), and read about Ruth Reichl's lifelong adventure with food. *Tender at the Bone: Growing Up at the Table* by Ruth Reichl.

ROMANCE

Definition: Simply put, a romance is a love story in which the focus is on the development of a relationship between main characters culminating in a happy ending. Romance is one of the largest genres, filled with seemingly unending subgenres. Fifty percent of all fiction paperback sales fit into this genre, which ranges from historical to contemporary, homosexual to heterosexual, steamy to gentle reads, realistic to supernatural, and much more. Despite the overwhelming variety within this genre, there are two elements that all romances have in common: first, the plot revolves around the love relationship of the main characters, and second, readers have a vested interest in the outcome of the romance.

Purpose: Provide readers with emotional involvement in the development of a love relationship. Readers should feel genuine satisfaction at the happy ending.

General Appeal Characteristics

Readers are drawn into the story to the extent that they experience vicarious pleasure from the characters' romantic involvement.

The plot contains some type of obstacle or barrier that the characters must overcome to reach a happy ending. These barriers could be physical, social, demographic, or moral, but they serve to create tension and yearning for the characters and readers.

Characters are well defined and easily identifiable. Men are strong, handsome (although there is a "beauty and the beast" subgenre), and often dangerous, misunderstood, or wronged in some fashion. Women are usually loyal and beautiful and can be either strong and independent or weak and needful of care and rescue.

Although there are densely written epic romance stories, romances are mainly quick reads that provide fast-paced pleasure, which can easily be stopped by interruptions and started again without loss of the story line.

Language is an important element in the romance novel. Long descriptive passages and heavy use of adjectives draw readers into the story and allow them to see the world and feel the emotions of the lovers. It is this connection between the story and the reader that defines a quality romance.

Samples

Match Me If You Can by Susan Elizabeth Phillips
New York: William Morrow, 2005
Romance, Humorous Fiction

Annabelle Granger has plans to become a successful businesswoman, and the first step is to take over her grandmother's matchmaking business. Now before you start humming that song from *Fiddler on the Roof*, let me say that matchmaking has come a long way. In order to make her business grow, Annabelle decides to snag the most eligible bachelor in Chicago as a client—then find him the perfect wife.

To that end, Annabelle sets up an appointment with Heath Champion, one of the top sports agents in the country. Heath has let it be known that he's ready to get married. Now, you may be wondering why he needs help in finding a wife. He's a gorgeous young multimillionaire who has his own table in all the hot spots in town. He's also, as Annabelle discovers, a demanding, controlling, overbearing, workalcoholic pain in the ... well, you know what I mean. He wants a wife who is beautiful, brilliant, cultured, and at his beck and call 24/7. To quote Heath: "She should be able to cook up a dinner for 20 of my football player clients with 30 minutes notice and be willing to drop everything to fly anywhere in the world with me to watch a game or entertain a potential client's wife or girlfriend."

This is impossible. Heath is impossible and he's driving Annabelle crazy, so how could she have fallen in love with him? How is she supposed to set him up with a bevy of brilliant beauties when she wants to be the only woman in his life? What happens when the matchmaker falls for her own client and how perfect does the perfect wife have to be?

Match Me If You Can, a modern romantic comedy by Susan Elizabeth Phillips.

* * *

The Trouble with Valentine's Day by Rachel Gibson
New York: Avon, 2005
Romance, Humorous Fiction

Kate thought she was going to faint. The buzzing in her ears grew louder and louder as the man she thought she would never see again appeared before her.

"Rob," said her grandfather. "Let me introduce you to Kate, my granddaughter from Las Vegas. I don't believe you've met."

Kate waited for Rob to indicate that on the contrary, they had met before. In fact, they met in a bar where Kate had invited him to see her tattoo, located in a very intimate place, and Rob had coldly rejected her. But Rob only held out his hand and allowed a small smile to show. "Nice to meet you, Kate," he said. "Are you in town long?"

Could it get much worse than this? First a commitment-phobic boyfriend made her question her love life. Then a bad experience at her investigative agency made her question her career path. Now Rob Sutter, former hockey player and one-night-stand decliner, lived in Gospel, Idaho—her new home. It was enough to make the strongest girl start to cry.

Kate clenched her teeth and shook Rob's hand. "Nice to meet you, Rob," she replied. "Any good bars in town?" *The Trouble with Valentine's Day* by Rachel Gibson.

*   *   *

The Good, the Bad, and the Ugly Men I've Dated by Shane Bolks
New York: Avon, 2005
Romance, Humorous Fiction

Rory Egglehoff has always been a dork. Beginning in the second grade, when she tripped and dropped all her books, she was too clumsy, too smart, and the class joke. On top of that, she's addicted to everything *Star Wars*, and has been since her parents took her to the first movie.

Now Rory's all grown up. She's an accountant, but she's still a dork who dates a geeky guy from work (whom her best friend calls Tedious Tom), and is still hopelessly addicted to *Star Wars*. Rory collects *Star Wars* memorabilia, attends conventions dressed as Princess Leia, and peppers her speech with phrases from the *Star Wars* series.

Rory's life changes when she runs into Hunter Chase (literally). Hunter is gorgeous, considerate, talented, athletic, successful, and sexy; the ultimate Jedi knight—and Rory has been in love with him since the second grade, when he picked up her books and didn't laugh at her.

Rory knows she doesn't stand a chance with Hunter. It would be a reverse version of *Beauty and the Beast*, and everyone knows that just doesn't happen in real life. However, her best friend, Allison, convinces Rory to launch a four-phase plan to get Hunter to not only notice her but to ask her to their high school reunion.

It seems impossible; Rory can barely speak when Hunter's in the room. Could she actually get him to notice her, to like her, to fall in love with her?

The Good, the Bad, and the Ugly Men I've Dated, a modern romantic fairy tale by Shane Bolks.

*   *   *

Something Borrowed by Emily Giffin
New York: St. Martin's, 2004
Romance

Meet Rachel White, the good girl. Rachel has always been the person who does the right thing in every situation. When work needs to be done, she goes into the office on the weekend. When her mother calls on the phone, she always answers. And when her best friend needs help with her upcoming wedding, Rachel is right there to help pick flower arrangements, try on bridal dresses, and sleep with the groom.

Wait a minute. Are we still talking about Rachel White, the good girl? The same girl who would never ever tell a lie, even if it was a teensy-weensy one? Are you saying she got drunk during her thirtieth birthday party, the one that her best friend, Darcy, planned for her, then slept with this same best friend's fiancé? Are we talking about that Rachel White?

Yes, we are. Meet Rachel White, wedding wrecker and slut. But let's give her some credit. She really didn't mean to sleep with her best friend's fiancé, and she had every intention of stopping things right there. Really, she did. But Marcus kept calling her and e-mailing her and before she knew it, she was seeing him on a regular basis at the same time she was planning to be the maid of honor at his wedding.

What will Rachel White, good girl slash wedding wrecker, do? Will she tell Darcy what she's been doing behind her back? Will she give Marcus an ultimatum and stick to it? Will she attend the wedding and watch the love of her life marry someone else? Rachel has some choices to make, including whether her own happiness is worth the price of someone else's joy. Rachel has borrowed something that doesn't belong to her; doing the right thing, whatever that is, won't be easy. *Something Borrowed* by Emily Giffin.

✳   ✳   ✳

The Mercy of Thin Air by Ronlyn Domingue
New York: Atria, 2005
Romance

Amy and Scott are in love. They have a beautiful marriage that combines moments of intense passion with an ongoing sense of belonging, ease, and comfort . . . until lately. They seem to have lost contact with each other. Scott still reaches out for Amy, but she's no longer there; somehow their connection has been broken.

Raziela and Andrew are also in love—or they were, until Raziela's unexpected, tragic death. But that was seventy years ago and time moves on, right? Well, not quite. Raziela decided not to move on. She's been living in the between—a realm that exists after life and before whatever lies beyond.

Over the years Raziela has lost track of Andrew but she's kept herself busy guiding other souls, living and dead. Now she haunts Amy and Scott's house and she notices that the once loving couple has lost their way. Can she help them find each other again? In helping Amy and Scott reignite their love will Raziela finally be able to come to terms with her own death and the tragic end of her great romance with Andrew?

The Mercy of Thin Air by Ronlyn Domingue is a gentle romance beautifully entwining two tragic love stories over seventy years. This debut novel will leave the reader gasping for breath and waiting for more.

✳   ✳   ✳

The Dark Queen by Susan Carroll
New York: Ballantine, 2005
Romance, Historical Fiction

Ariane Cheney is late for her own wedding and she doesn't even care. Of course, the fact that the Comte de Renard never properly asked her might have something to do with it, but in reality she has something far more important to do. An injured man has shown up with incriminating evidence against the Dark Queen, Catherine de Medici.

Ariane is one of a long line of women known as the Daughters of the Earth. At first they were revered for their wisdom and knowledge with healing and white magic, but now men are afraid of their power and have outlawed their practices. It's long been rumored that the Dark Queen practices black magic and has been trying to incriminate the Daughters so they cannot practice their good magic against her bad. Ariane must do whatever she can to save herself and her sisters from the Dark Queen, even if it means she has to join forces with the wretched Comte de Renard. The only way he'll help her is if she promises to marry him, a bargain she takes with no intention of honoring.

It truly irks Ariane that she has to accept help from an overbearing oaf like Renard, but the future of her people depends on it. If only she could stop thinking about his handsome face when she closes her eyes at night, everything would work out fine. *The Dark Queen* by Susan Carroll.

*   *   *

Hotel Transylvania by Chelsea Quinn Yarbro
New York: St. Martin's, 1978
Romance, Chiller, Historical Fiction

Madelaine de Montalia is young, beautiful, and naive. Raised in a convent in the country, she is thrilled to experience her first trip to Paris. Not only will Madelaine get to stay with her wealthy and doting aunt, she will be introduced to all best families and discover, firsthand, the lavish parties, luxurious lifestyle, and unending privileges enjoyed by the members of the court of Louis XV.

The main purpose of Madelaine's visit is to find a suitable husband, and she knows that the social engagements she loves are the perfect opportunity for her to meet and impress the titled bachelors of France. Madelaine soon becomes discouraged as she discovers that the eligible men she meets are either old, young and stupid, or have been involved in scandals of such magnitude that their last hope of redemption is to marry a woman of impeccable breeding with an unquestionably spotless reputation.

There is only one man who doesn't fall into one of these categories, the mysterious Comte de Saint-Germain. Here is a man with a quick wit and sharp mind whose boundless curiosity rivals Madelaine's own. Saint-Germain admires Madelaine's intelligence and forthright manner. He sympathizes with her boredom of the endless, mindless chatter, the pomp and protocol of court. Although he's older than Madelaine, Saint-Germain never treats her like a child. His manner is gentle but never condescending. Before she knows it, she has fallen deeply in love with the suave and debonair comte.

There's just one problem: Saint-Germain is a vampire. Is Madelaine's love deep enough to overcome her fear of becoming one of the undead? When a titled suitor puts into motion a sinister plan to capture Madelaine and involve her in the fiendish plans of his evil circle of friends, will Saint-Germain be willing to risk everything to save the woman who has captured his heart?

Hotel Transylvania, a novel of forbidden love by Chelsea Quinn Yarbro.

*   *   *

The Spy's Kiss by Nita Abrams
New York: Zebra, 2005
Romance, Historical Fiction

Serena Allen knows she has a temper. All the women in her family do. She also knows that she tends to be a tad too cynical, especially when it comes to men. She had to learn the hard way that men can't be trusted; her reputation was ruined after her fiancé left her in a compromising position before their wedding. So when Julien Clermont shows up at her aunt and uncle's country estate to study a butterfly collection, she is immediately suspicious. Sure, Julien is charming and handsome. Sure, he's rich and titled. Sure, he seems to like Serena, despite her scandalous past. But she doesn't believe for one minute he's interested in some old bugs with wings. She really thinks he's a spy for France trying to steal some important documents given to her uncle for safekeeping, and no amount of matchmaking by her aunt is going to make her change her mind.

What Serena and her family don't know is that Julien is indeed on a top-secret mission. Like Serena, Julien was also involved in a scandal, though not of his own making, and he is determined to find the culprit. Little does he know that there is another spy amongst the family, all too willing to let Julien take the blame for his misdeeds. Can Serena put aside her distrust in order to save him from almost certain death? The Spy's Kiss may convince her to do just that. . . . *The Spy's Kiss* by Nita Abrams.

SCIENCE FICTION

Definition: Is it science fiction or fantasy? This is a question that has plagued librarians and readers since the genre began. At the Arizona Library Association Annual Conference one year, author Orson Scott Card was asked the difference between science fiction and fantasy. His answer: "Look at the cover. If it has rivets it's science fiction, if it has trees it's fantasy!" For many, a more concrete definition is that science fiction titles rely on science, not magic, to create locations and characters that interact with their world.

Subjects covered in this genre include time travel, space travel, aliens, other worlds, inventions, alternate histories, and past or future civilizations. Fantasy is comprised of magical places, beings, or abilities, as well as mythical or imaginary creatures or locations.

Purpose: Offers readers an intellectual and diverse universe to explore and conquer while providing speculative and surprising answers to questions such as "What if . . . ?" "How about . . . ?" or "If only . . ." Readers' minds are unbound by the constraints of current reality and are free to experience, imagine, and believe in anything.

General Appeal Characteristics

Science fiction provides readers with an intellectual escape from reality. Fans of this genre take pride in their belief that the inventions, journeys, settings, and experiences found in these books are not only possible but attainable—if only in the distant future.

Setting is an important element of the story. Science fiction relies heavily on technical and scientific details, real or imaginary, to create the location, time, and tone of the novel.

Science fiction is a genre that lends itself to series. Readers who enjoy a particular character or setting will often be able to look forward to future installments in a series.

Although characters are often secondary to either the setting or science, they are well defined and believable. Consistency in physical descriptions, personality traits, and tone are keys to creating well-rounded science fiction characters.

Samples

In the Garden of Iden by Kage Baker
New York: Harcourt Brace, 1997
Science Fiction

Once upon a time in the future, a group of scientists and merchants figured out how to be immortal, travel back in time, improve the human condition, and make a lot of money at the same time. Of course, all of this took a lot of experimenting and testing and mistakes before they discovered the first rule of time travel: recorded history cannot be changed. In other words, you can't loot the future, but you can loot the past.

After the Company, as this group came to be known, became very wealthy and influential, someone remembered that they had wanted to make the world a better place. So they sent agents back in time to collect extinct animals and long-forgotten medicinal plants that cured diseases and stuff. But the time travel agents started getting cranky. They didn't like traveling back in time to dirty, smelly, disease-infected places. It just wasn't fun anymore.

So the Company started collecting children to be time travel agents, since their small brains could be reconstructed into cyborgs with the fewest side effects. That's where Mendoza comes in. Trained to be a botanist, Mendoza's first trip back through time is to the England of 1554, assigned to collect a type of holly that can cure cancer in the twenty-fourth century. Posing as a Spanish lady accompanying her doctor father, she falls in love with a mortal man, which is a big no-no in time travel. Their love affair puts the whole mission in jeopardy and causes Mendoza to choose between her task and her love, with disastrous results. *In the Garden of Iden* by Kage Baker.

✳ ✳ ✳

Doomsday Book by Connie Willis
New York: Bantam, 1992
Science Fiction, Historical Fiction

In the year 2048, historians are not limited to books, journals, and dusty old documents. When they want to know about a period in history, they just send someone back in time to learn firsthand what life was like. Of course, it's not that easy. It would be disastrous if someone discovered that you were from the future; it could be deadly. There are also the dangers inherent to each time period. For instance, no one is allowed to attempt time travel to the Middle Ages; what with the wars and plague, it's just too risky.

Unfortunately, Professor Gilchrist has other ideas. Time travel is so common that it has become boring. But time travel to an age that's never been explored before—that would be something. That would generate new interest in his work, put him at the top of the promotion list. He's determined to send a historian back to the Middle Ages.

The plan is daring; the plan is ruthless; okay—the plan is stupid! Safety corners have been cut and Gilchrist uses an undergraduate student with no time travel experience. Yes, Kivrin volunteered to go, and, since she's set to go back to 1320, more than twenty years before the Black Death reached England, she's sure she'll be fine, right? *Wrong!*

Unexplainably, Kivrin loses consciousness during the time travel and awakens to discover that she's dressed all wrong, she's lost, and worst of all, she's terribly ill. Kivrin soon discovers that there was an error in the calculations. She's been sent back to the Middle Ages, all right, but not to 1320. She finds herself in England in 1348, an England dying of bubonic plague.

Rich with details and descriptions of daily life, *Doomsday Book* by Connie Willis is a must-read for anyone who loves historical fiction!

✳ ✳ ✳

Archangel by Sharon Shinn
New York: Ace, 1996
Science Fiction, Romance

Gabriel is soon to be archangel, leader of the host of angels who watch over the planet Samaria. The law of Jovah states, however, that first he must find and marry the woman chosen to be his wife. All he knows about her is that she's twenty-five years old, she's a farmer's daughter, and her name is Rachel. That's it. And Gabriel has only six months to find her before the Gloria, the annual gathering to praise Jehovah, but he's not worried. All little girls grow up dreaming of becoming the angelica and standing beside the archangel to lead the multitude in song. He knows she'll be so pleased and honored to be chosen that the whole business will be done with as little fuss as possible.

But Gabriel soon learns that it is not easy to locate Rachel. Her village has been destroyed and her family killed. Her Kiss, a jewel-like device implanted in all babies dedicated to the god, indicates that she lives, but where? When he attends a wedding at a wealthy landowner's home, he notices his own Kiss burns and changes colors every time a certain slave woman lights the morning fire in his room. Yes, the slave is Rachel, who surprises Gabriel by having absolutely no interest in becoming the new angelica or having anything to do with this moody, arrogant creature who thinks he's god's gift to mortal women everywhere.

How can two individuals who dislike each other so much join together to save the people of Samaria? Gabriel and Rachel are the planet's only hope. *Archangel* by Sharon Shinn.

*   *   *

The Eyre Affair by Jasper Fforde
New York: Viking, 2002
Science Fiction

Thursday Next comes from an unusual family. Her father is wanted by the police for excessive time travel, her mother raises dodos, and her uncle Mycroft has invented a machine that allows people to pop into books and interact with the characters.

Acheron Hades is listed as the third most evil man in England. He is a vicious killer who enjoys murder as much as some people enjoy ice cream. He takes pride in the fact that he is totally without a conscience and he has developed certain abilities that make it almost impossible to capture or contain him. What abilities? you ask. Well, he can hear if anyone says his name within a fifty-mile radius, he can control your mind, he can walk through glass, he is invisible to all cameras (video or still), and he can be shot at point-blank range and walk away unharmed.

How are Thursday and Acheron connected? Acheron has used his special powers to steal the original manuscript of *Jane Eyre* and has also kidnapped Mycroft and stolen his machine. With it, he has entered the manuscript and kidnapped Jane. Since *Jane Eyre* is written in the first person, when Jane is kidnapped the novel ends. And since he took her from the manuscript, every edition ever published also ends. Acheron vows to kill Jane and to continue to steal and change manuscripts unless his demands are met.

It's up to Thursday to rescue her uncle, restore Jane to her story, and capture Acheron before the world's greatest works of literature are destroyed forever in *The Eyre Affair*, the first in a series by Jasper Fforde.

✳   ✳   ✳

Beggars in Spain by Nancy Kress
New York: William Morrow, 1993
Science Fiction

Shopping for a baby? How about a custom order—a baby made just for you? Green eyes, blond hair, musical? Tall? Slender? Super intelligent? Sleeping or nonsleeping?

That's right. It's the twenty-first century and genetic engineering has made it possible for those who can afford it to custom-order their babies. Leisha Camden, the daughter of a wealthy industrialist, is one of these new prodigies who spend their nights awake while the whole family snoozes away for eight hours. But she doesn't just watch TV or read a book. No, her father has hired special teachers for her, so Leisha can learn more and more all night long. All this extra time naturally leads to high productivity, and these sleepless children start to accomplish some pretty amazing things.

Soon the sleepers begin to resent those who don't sleep. Every night there are reports about laws that discriminate against the sleepless, even making sex between sleepers and sleepless a third-degree felony. To escape the increasing violence, the sleepless retreat to an armed camp called the Sanctuary, where they attempt to live in freedom. But when they start to reproduce, creating their own superbabies, the sleepless discover that repression and discrimination are not limited to world of the sleepers. *Beggars in Spain* by Nancy Kress.

✳   ✳   ✳

Childhood's End by Arthur C. Clarke
New York: Ballantine, 1953
Science Fiction

Earth is on the brink of destroying itself. War, pollution, disease—the problems seem insurmountable—until the day the Overlords come.

That's what we call them. We don't know what they call themselves. Their huge spaceships encircle the earth, hovering high above all major cities.

The Overlords are advanced, secretive, and powerful. No one knows what they look like, where they come from, or what they're doing here.

They say they just want to help, to make Earth a paradise again. And during the fifty years that they've been here, they have done amazing things. The impenetrable barriers they gave to every country have eliminated war. Most diseases have been cured, and they even got rid of rush-hour traffic! And the way they got us to stop hurting animals . . . let's just say there won't be another bullfight any time soon.

Now, I hate to look a gift alien in the mouth, but things aren't always what they seem. The Overlords have another purpose—a mission that will determine the fate of humankind—and every scientist who comes close to figuring it out mysteriously disappears. Have we become too complacent? Is it too late, or will we survive? *Childhood's End* by Arthur C. Clarke.

                          *   *   *

The Man Who Fell to Earth by Walter Tevis
New York: Laurel Leaf, 1963
Science Fiction

Thomas Jerome Newton is rich, very rich. He's "I won the Powerball" rich. He owns and operates World Enterprises Corporation, which holds the patents on all his new inventions. He's made hundreds of millions of dollars on his new designs for Worldcolor film, televisions, amplifiers, fuel, and so much more. His inventions have revolutionized the entertainment industry. He's looked at as a combination of Albert Einstein, Thomas Edison, and Howard Hughes. Everyone knows that he's a genius. Most people agree that he's an odd, shy, eccentric little man.

He seems to have only two friends, Betty Jo and Bryce, two people as different as they could be: one an uneducated drunk, the other a retired college professor. Both of them are vital to Thomas Jerome Newton, but only one knows what his plans are, only one knows why he needs all that money— only one knows that he's an alien. *The Man Who Fell to Earth* by Walter Tevis.

                          *   *   *

The Terrorists of Irustan by Louise Marley
New York: Ace, 1999
Science Fiction, Women's Fiction

From the Book of the Second Prophet:

"The Maker chose to make man larger, stronger, and wiser than woman. Husbands must be responsible for their wives, for their sustenance, their clothing, their shelter, their well-being, and their discipline, according to the guidance of the One."

On Irustan, the Book of the Second Prophet is the first authority for all behavior. The second authority is the husband. Each man has total control over every woman in his household, from his wife to his daughters to the lowest servant. Men do not heal the sick and don't like talking about medical conditions. The Book of the Second Prophet says this is so.

On Irustan, women cover every inch of their body when in public, using three veils to cover their faces. They are not allowed to speak directly to any male but their husband and servants. Women are the healers and the only ones allowed to touch sick people. The Book of the Second Prophet says this is so.

On Irustan, Zahra is a young female medicant, or healer, who sees too many abused women and children in her clinic. She decides that the only way to make things right is to murder those men who treat their wives and daughters so cruelly. Soon the men start to wonder why so many are dying.

On Irustan, one woman does have the power to change things. Even if the Book of the Second Prophet doesn't say this is so. *The Terrorists of Irustan* by Louise Marley.

SEA ADVENTURES

Definition: This is actually a subgenre of the larger adventure genre. Sea adventures are stories of an individual or group that experience danger or must overcome obstacles while accomplishing some task or mission on or under the sea. Sea adventures can take place in any time period or setting, real or imagined.

Purpose: Provide the reader with opportunities to vicariously experience dangers and accomplish heroic tasks in often exotic settings.

General Appeal Characteristics

The story focuses on action, physical danger, obstacles, and heroic accomplishments.

There is always an easily identifiable leader/hero whom readers like and can relate to and cheer for. Whether male or female, this hero utilizes skill, quick wit, and ingenuity to accomplish the task and save the day.

Locations are often exotic and provide hidden challenges for the hero to overcome, allowing readers to experience a place it would often be impossible to visit in reality.

Pacing is fast and furious; this is an action-packed thrill ride. Although setting details are important, readers don't want to get bogged down in page after page of description.

The ending is either a happy one where the hero is triumphant, or a cliffhanger that leaves readers on the edge of their seats, eagerly waiting for the next installment in the series.

Samples

The Blackbirder by James Nelson
New York: William Morrow, 2001
Sea Adventure, Historical Fiction

Thomas Marlowe is a gentleman and his wife, Elizabeth, is a lady. They are landowners and churchgoers in Virginia. It's very important that you remember this because if you happen to mention that Thomas used to be a pirate and Elizabeth used to be a prostitute, Thomas will kill you.

When Thomas was a pirate he sailed with men of all colors, and men were judged by how well they worked, not the color of their skin. So when Thomas became a landowner, despite the strong objections of his neighbors, he freed all the slaves who came with the plantation and hired them back and paid them as you would any free workers.

Thomas's right-hand man is a former slave named King James who one day succumbs to a fit of rage, kills a white man, and escapes to the sea.

Now we've got trouble. Using this as proof that slaves should never be freed or treated like "regular" human beings, Thomas's neighbors try to force the governor to seize all of his property and wealth.

The governor gives Thomas one chance to make things right. He must bring King James back to stand trial. Everyone knows the trial will be a farce, and that no matter the provocation, King James will be hanged for killing a white man. But Thomas has no choice. He could easily give up all his land and go back to being a pirate, but he can't let anyone destroy the life of respectability he has built for Elizabeth.

So the hunt is on. Both men are expert sailors, both men excel in combat, and both men know that only one will come out of this alive. *The Blackbirder* by James Nelson.

* * *

Wake of the Perdido Star by Gene Hackman and Daniel Lenihan
New York: Newmarket, 1999
Sea Adventure, Historical Fiction

Black Jack is the fiercest pirate sailing the South Seas, and men quake at the very mention of his name. As the leader of a renegade sailing ship called the *Perdido Star*, he has become known for his daring adventures and quick action against those who threaten him.

But Jack wasn't always the pirate known as Black Jack. He began his life on the sea when he was seventeen, on his way to Cuba with his parents. Instead of the welcome home they had expected, Jack's parents were murdered in cold blood, with Jack as the only witness. Not knowing what else to do, he signed on as a crew member of the *Perdido Star* and made the sea his new home. But he never forgot what happened to his parents, and he vowed to avenge their deaths if it was the last thing he ever did.

It has taken him several years, but he finally has enough men, firearms, and information to follow through with the plan that has consumed his every waking minute: Killing the man who murdered his parents. Never forgetting the vow he made at seventeen, Jack brings the *Perdido Star* back to Cuba for revenge, but he discovers that his own obsession with blood puts the whole crew in danger. *Wake of the Perdido Star* by Gene Hackman and Daniel Lenihan.

*   *   *

The Iron Rose by Marsha Canham
New York: Signet, 2003
Sea Adventure, Romance, Historical Fiction

Take one beautiful young woman who can beat any man in a swordfight and has her own pirate ship. Add one stuffy yet extremely handsome Duke of Harrow, who has been sent by King James on a mission. Mix in some swashbuckling battles, a few heaving bosoms, and a dash of heavy antagonism—and what do you get? A lusty sea adventure romance.

Juliet Dante is the daughter of the feared pirate Simon Dante, who has roamed the Caribbean for years raiding and pillaging Spanish riches. Although young and lovely to look at, Juliet is a fierce fighter and a skilled sailor in her own right. When she encounters a British ship being attacked by a Spanish galleon, she wastes no time coming to its aid—and to the aid of the sexy and strong Varian St. Clare. But he is injured, so she brings him aboard her ship, the *Iron Rose*, to nurse him back to health. Too bad his clothes have all been ruined and he has to recuperate naked in her cabin, since that seems to cause quite a distraction for the ship's captain.

It must be the fresh ocean breezes that kindle something between Juliet and Varian—or is it just too many lonely days at sea? Whatever the cause, this rollicking love story would make great beach reading on a hot summer day. *The Iron Rose* by Marsha Canham.

*   *   *

The Captain's Wife by Douglas Kelley
New York: Dutton, 2001
Sea Adventure, Historical Fiction

Mary Patton is nineteen and in love. Her husband, Joshua, is everything she ever dreamed of: strong, handsome, virile, and, at twenty-nine, one of the youngest captains of the mighty clipper ships.

Mary is about to go on the adventure of a lifetime as she sails around the world with her husband on his ship, *Neptune's Car*. She's sailed before; on the last voyage she even learned how to use the sextant to pass the time (much to her husband's amusement).

Most of the crew was on the last voyage. The only new member is the first mate, Mr. Keeler, a last-minute addition. He doesn't have a good reputation, but Mary has total faith in her husband's ability to keep the crew in line.

Things go wrong from the beginning. Every time Mr. Keeler is left in charge the sails are drawn in and the course is slightly altered, dramatically slowing the progress the ship makes each day. Joshua talks to him over and over, but nothing seems to work and Mary watches helplessly as her husband grows more and more frustrated with his recalcitrant first mate.

Disaster strikes when Mr. Keeler attempts to lead the crew in mutiny, attacking Joshua before he can be thwarted and chained in the cargo hold. Joshua regains control and things seem to be better when he is struck with a mysterious illness, lapsing into a coma and leaving *Neptune's Car* without a first mate or a captain.

Second mate Mr. Hare is willing to take command of the ship until the captain's recovery, but there are two problems: first, he can't read, write, or use the sextant, so he can't navigate; and second, they're headed for the treacherous passage of Cape Horn, which is experiencing its most devastating weather in years.

Mary can navigate, but the question is: Will the crew be led by a woman, or will they succumb to the promises of Mr. Keeler who assures them that he will see the ship safely to shore if they set him free?

Based on a true story, *The Captain's Wife* by Douglas Kelley is a thrilling tale of love, faith, and courage.

                          *   *   *

The Magnificent Savages by Fred Mustard Stewart
New York: Forge, 1996
Sea Adventure, Historical Fiction

At twelve years old, Justin Savage is the apple of his father's eye, despite the fact that he's the result of a shocking love affair and therefore illegitimate. His father, Nathanial Savage, has always done whatever he wanted, even though scandal followed the family. But as one of the richest men in New York and owner of a fleet of clipper ships, Nathanial has never cared what people thought. So he brought Justin up to love sailing and the wide ocean seas, in order to be useful wherever the family business took him.

But Nathanial is ill now and the end is near. Before he dies, Nathanial arranges for Justin to ship out aboard the *Sea Witch* as a cabin boy. He will be the lowest of the low, expected to do all the dirty jobs no one else wants to do. Still, he's ready and eager to begin his new life, never suspecting that his older half brother, Sylvaner, has other plans for him. Sylvaner has always been jealous of Justin, and he wants to make sure he is the only heir when his father dies. As Justin boards the *Sea Witch*, little does he know that one of the members of the crew is a hired killer just waiting for the perfect opportunity to make Sylvaner an only child once again. *The Magnificent Savages* by Fred Mustard Stewart.

* * *

Life of Pi by Yann Martel
New York: Harcourt, 2001
Sea Adventure, Multicultural Fiction

Pi Patel has questions. His family is Hindu . . . why? Would they be different if they were Muslim, Jewish, or Christian? What is the difference? His father is a zookeeper in India, so Pi has been around animals all his life. Do animals have religion? Why do people hurt animals? Why are they moving the zoo from India to Canada? How do you survive a shipwreck in a lifeboat with a hungry Bengal tiger?

Didn't expect that last question, did you? This is *Life of Pi* by Yann Martel, a humorous drama that challenges you to ponder life's biggest questions while providing a rip-roaring ride full of plot twists with an ending that will leave you gasping for breath. One warning, if you're one of those people who read the end of the book first, don't!

* * *

The Voyage of the Narwhal by Andrea Barrett
New York: Norton, 1998
Sea Adventure, Historical Fiction

The crew aboard the *Narwhal* is confused. Why on earth are they going to the arctic north so late in the season? Zeke, the commander of the expedition, assures the captain that they'll be back before the ice sets in, but Zeke keeps pushing them to go farther and farther north to discover something called an open polar sea. The crew has never seen such a thing and doesn't believe it even exists.

Despite objections, Zeke orders the crew to explore an uncharted area, and before they know it, the ship is stuck fast in the ice. This means they have to spend the long, cold Arctic winter aboard the ship until the ice breaks up and they can start the journey home. When the weather warms up, the crew is astonished when Zeke orders the captain to proceed north again instead of going home. It appears that Zeke is more concerned about his own fame and fortune than the crew's safety.

How can the crew survive another winter in the frozen Arctic when it's so cold that the men's beards freeze to their neckerchiefs and frozen saliva seals their lips shut? They have no food, no supplies, and no energy left for another long winter. When Zeke refuses to listen to reason and the ship becomes stuck in the ice again, the crew decides it's time to take matters into their own hands. *The Voyage of the Narwhal* by Andrea Barrett.

* * *

Star of the Sea by Joseph O'Connor
Orlando: Harcourt, 2002
Sea Adventure, Historical Fiction

Okay, here's the picture: It's 1847 and you're in Ireland, where thousands are starving to death because of the potato famine. Your only hope is to sail to America. You work and save, but there's just no money to be had so you finally sell yourself into indentured servitude for your one chance to escape the horror that Ireland has become.

Your ship is the *Star of the Sea* and it's beautiful—richly decorated, filled with delicate crystal and china, and overflowing with delicious, exotic food. But only for those in first class. Theirs is a world of servants, fine clothes, soft beds, and clean fresh air. Yours is the world of steerage—of rats, disease, starvation, and death. As the rich gorge themselves on fine foods and dance the night away you try to survive on the one piece of hardtack and cup of water that you're given each day as you struggle to breathe in the putrid, fetid hold that you're confined to.

You dream of making it in America, of some day having the life of ease that exists above you. But there's one passenger who isn't dreaming of being rich, he's dreaming of getting his vengeance on the rich.

The *Star of the Sea* is sailing toward the New World and there's a serial killer on board. *Star of the Sea* by Joseph O'Connor.

WOMEN'S FICTION

Definition: Women's fiction delves into the issues, relationships, and lives of women. These novels can be set in any location, culture, or time period, and can involve women of any demographic group. These books don't always have happy endings, but they do always reach a resolution.

Purpose: Allows readers to explore, ponder, or relate to the issues, relationships, situations, and emotions of women. This genre can act to provide readers with insight into an issue or situation, provide an emotional outlet by enabling readers to relate to a variety of events or concerns, or act as a trusted friend, allowing readers to question their thoughts, opinions, or feelings.

General Appeal Characteristics

The main character is female. Secondary characters are important to the story and are also usually female. The majority of books in this genre are written by women; because of this, female readers feel a kinship with the author and believe that the author understands, respects, and admires women.

Story lines are realistic and deal with situations faced by real women. Readers can relate to the characters and what they're going through and either have or can develop a personal understanding of the characters' lives and situations. Relationships, whether with friends, family, lovers, or antagonists, play a vital role in the story line. Although the ending isn't always happy or the one that is most desired, there is a final resolution to the issues raised in the story.

Because both the author and readers are usually women, the language of this genre has an intimate feel to it that is lacking in many other genres. It's as if the reader and author belong to a secret club, which enables them to express themselves freely without needing to justify themselves or explain their meaning.

Samples

Sight Hound by Pam Houston
New York: Norton, 2005
Women's Fiction

Rae and Dante have been together a long time and are totally attached to each other. Rae is the human who loves Dante so much that she will do anything to keep him with her, despite the cancer that took his leg and threatens his life. Dante is the Irish wolfhound who is trying to stay alive long enough to help her find another human who will love her properly after he's gone. That human looks like it just might be Howard, an actor who's in love with Rae. Dante isn't sure, but he thinks that Howard just might be good enough to take over the job of showing Rae how much she deserves to be loved.

It's funny how love is both harder, and easier, without language. Rae is surrounded by people and animals who love her, but nothing compares to the bond she has with Dante. Dante is both wise and gentle; he quotes Buddha and understands far more about life than most people. Rae has spent her whole life convinced that the one sure way not to get what she wants is to hope for it. Dante is spending his whole life trying to show her that love is stronger than fear. Together they create a remarkable and unforgettable story that readers will remember a long time afterward. *Sight Hound* by Pam Houston.

*   *   *

Gods in Alabama by Joshilyn Jackson
New York: Warner, 2005
Women's Fiction

People from small towns in Alabama know that there is more than one God; in fact, there are several. There's the high school quarterback, trucks, large-breasted women, Jim Beam, and, of course, Jesus. Arlene Fleet is very familiar with the gods in Alabama. She is from one of these small towns; she was raised in tiny Possett. When Arlene graduated from high school and moved to Chicago she made three promises to God (the real one) and she only asked him for one thing in return. She promised not to lie, not to have any more sex outside marriage, and never, no matter what, to return home to Possett, Alabama.

It's been twelve years and Arlene has kept her word. First, she has never lied. She may not tell the whole truth, but she doesn't lie. Once she even cleaned out her bank account so she could honestly tell her mother she didn't have the money to go home for a visit. Second, even though she's deeply in love with Burr, she hasn't had sex in twelve years! Third, no matter how much her mother pleads and her aunt Florence threatens, she hasn't gone back to Alabama.

As far as Arlene is concerned, she's more than kept her side of the bargain, so why didn't God keep his? All he had to do was make sure that no one found out that when she was fifteen years old she murdered her high school's quarterback. Is that too much to ask?

Gods in Alabama, an exciting debut novel by Joshilyn Jackson.

*   *   *

Good in Bed by Jennifer Weiner
New York: Pocket Books, 2001
Women's Fiction, Humor

One morning while Cannie Shapiro is at work, her best friend calls her up in a panic and instructs her to run down to the newsstand and buy the latest issue of *Moxie*, a contemporary fashion magazine. Her panic makes Cannie panic, so she drops everything to buy the magazine and a package of chocolate M&Ms to cope with this sudden emergency. When she gets back, her friend tells her to turn to page 132 and read the article titled "Good in Bed," a regular feature in the magazine. At first, Cannie's eyes don't seem to make sense of the letters, but then they focus and she sees the words in big black letters—"Loving a Larger Woman," by Bruce Guberman—and she chokes on her candy. Bruce Guberman had been her boyfriend, once, until she broke up with him. And now he's written an article about her in which the first line is, "I'll never forget the day I found out my girlfriend weighed more than I did."

Suddenly, Cannie has a hard time breathing, and her friend, still on the phone, sounds very far away. This is the most shocking and humiliating thing that has ever happened to her. Everyone she knows reads *Moxie*, and sure enough, soon the phone calls start and she goes into exile in her apartment. The only way she can think of to cope with something like this is to drink too many margaritas, curse Bruce vehemently, and generally wallow in self-pity. Then, feeling slightly hung over, she uses the situation to make some new resolutions for changing her life. She joins a weight loss group, makes some new friends, and discovers that a horrible situation can bring about one of the most exciting, rewarding, and wildly amusing years of her life. *Good in Bed* by Jennifer Weiner.

*   *   *

Angry Housewives Eating Bon Bons by Lorna Landvik
New York: Ballantine, 2003
Women's Fiction

Faith is new to Freesia Court and the unbearably cold Minnesota winter. Her husband, an airline pilot, is often away and she is lonely. She used to be so energetic and involved, but now, trapped in this frozen wasteland, she feels isolated and miserable.

All that changes one dark and snowy evening in March. Who could have guessed that one night would change her life forever, but that's just what happened that night—the night the power went out—the night she met her neighbors:

Kari: the oldest, a widow with a flair for sewing whose easy, heartwarming laugh hides a secret desire;
Slip: a boisterous revolutionary who juggles her family, friends, and causes with ease, and who never lets her diminutive size stop her from trying to change the world;
Merit: young, beautiful, and soft-spoken, a doctor's wife whose house and life appear to be perfect;
and Audrey: the neighborhood sexpot with a heart of gold who talks big but is completely devoted to her husband and children, whose brains and breeding help them all get through the bad times.

The five of them form a book club to share their love of reading. They meet each month to discuss a book, but it becomes so much more. Over thirty years, with equal parts of humor and strength, they share their thoughts, feelings, and lives in *Angry Housewives Eating Bon Bons* by Lorna Landvik.

*   *   *

My Sister's Keeper by Jodi Picoult
New York: Atria, 2004
Women's Fiction

Anna is thirteen years old and has undergone more surgeries, blood transfusions, shots, and tests than most people have in their whole lifetime. You would think that Anna has cancer, maybe, or some other terrible disease—but you would be wrong. Anna's not sick. The sick one is her sister, Kate, who was diagnosed with acute leukemia when she was two years old, before Anna was even born. Anna owes her very existence to Kate, because Anna was created to be a perfect genetic match in order to save her sister's life. Whenever Kate needs stem cells or bone marrow to fight off the cancer, it's Anna who provides them. Nearly every time Kate is hospitalized, Anna is, too. But now that Anna is thirteen, she is tired of all the tests, the transfusions, the procedures. So she gathers her life savings of one hundred thirty six dollars and eighty-seven cents and visits a lawyer in order to sue her parents for the rights to her own body. She knows this will disrupt her family and interrupt her sister's treatment. She knows her parents will be angry with her. She even realizes that it could become a media circus, but she doesn't care. She may owe her very existence to her sister, but now it's time to finally have a life of her own. *My Sister's Keeper* by Jodi Picoult.

*   *   *

The Yokota Officers Club by Sarah Bird
New York: Knopf, 2001
Women's Fiction

Everyone's heard of "military brats"—kids who live on military bases, who move from one exotic location to the next, and who get away with murder because they're an "officer's kid." But nobody talks about how hard it is to always be the new kid in school or about the pressure. Get away with murder? Hah! If they only knew!

In the military, when your father's an officer, everything you do reflects on him and his career, so if you mess up, he could be the one in trouble. It works like this: if you're not a good kid, he's not a good father. If he's not a good father, he can't be a good officer, and if he's not a good officer he gets passed over come promotion time.

This is the real world of an officer's kid—the world of Bernadette "Bernie" Root and her five brothers and sisters. Bernie's father is an officer in the US Air Force, a pilot who is always away on missions and who loves flying more than breathing. It's not that he doesn't love his family—he does, it's just that he expects so much. He wants everything and everyone to be perfect!

Bernie's mother understands the pressure her children are under and uses her endless energy and charm to ease their way. While they were stationed at the Yokota Air Base near Tokyo, she was always coming up with kooky ideas to turn the Officers Club into their own private playground. As a child, when her father was away, Bernie's life was filled with music and laughter.

So it's a total shock when Bernie returns home after finishing her first year in college, and sees the changes in her family. Yes, they've moved again and the base in Okinawa is kind of dumpy. But what's happened to everyone? Her father is never home, her mother barely gets out of bed anymore, her brothers and sisters mope around all day, and the house is a mess!

Bernie's determined to find out what went wrong. The once-noisy house has become secretive and sullen. No one will discuss what happened. The only thing Bernie knows is that whatever it is, it happened at the Yokota Officers Club. *The Yokota Officers Club* by Sarah Bird.

* * *

Good Grief by Lolly Winston
New York: Warner, 2004
Women's Fiction, Humor

Sophie Stanton is thirty-six years old and misses her husband terribly. Even though Ethan died of cancer three months ago, Sophie is having some problems processing her grief and seems to be stuck in the "eating Oreos in bed" stage. She really wants to be the Jackie Kennedy kind of widow—you know, the slim, composed woman who manages to be elegant and graceful while in mourning. Unfortunately, she is more of the Jack Daniel's type of widow—she eats too much, has trouble remembering to shower, and can't bear to get rid of her husband's clothes when Goodwill comes to collect them.

Sophie would really like to get on with her life—really, she would—but it's getting harder and harder to get out of bed each morning. She wishes there was a book to help with this, like an *Idiot's Guide to Grief*, or *Denial for Dummies*. It isn't until she goes to work one day wearing her nightgown and bunny slippers that someone notices her condition and does something about it—besides firing her, of course. That someone is Ruth, her best friend, who convinces her to get rid of Ethan's things, sell her house, and move to Oregon to live with Ruth for a while. Ruth and Sophie have been friends forever and know each other better than anyone. Sophie knows that Ruth will help her get over losing Ethan. She will help Sophie figure out a new life in Oregon, a new life without Ethan, a new life that allows her to be herself. *Good Grief* by Lolly Winston.

* * *

Ahab's Wife, or, The Star-Gazer by Sena Jeter Naslund
New York: William Morrow, 1999
Women's Fiction, Historical Fiction

"Captain Ahab was neither my first husband nor my last." Thus begins the unforgettable life story of Una Spenser.

Una is cursed: She has a sharp mind, a curious nature, and an unbreakable spirit, but she was born female and society says she should be content to sit coyly on the sidelines. Una would rather die. She is determined to live her life as she sees fit.

At twelve she's forced to leave home to escape the beatings her father feels will correct her willful behavior. At sixteen she disguises herself as a boy and joins the crew of the whaling ship the *Sussex*. Lost at sea and forced to resort to desperate measures to survive, Una first encounters the *Pequod* and its mighty Captain Ahab.

This sweeping epic takes you on a roller-coaster ride from the mountains of West Virginia to the vastness of the ocean as Una experiences all that life has to offer in this rich saga inspired by a single line from the classic *Moby-Dick*. *Ahab's Wife, or, The Star-Gazer* by Sena Jeter Naslund.

BOOKTALKS BY GENRE

We have found that often a single title can fit into multiple genres and be utilized for a variety of programs on different themes. For example, the sample booktalk for *Hotel Transylvania* is listed under romantic fiction, but it could also be used in a program of chillers or historical fiction. To enable you to easily identify all the books that could fit into each section we have provided this index of titles by genre.

Chillers

Belladonna
Five Mile House
Hotel Transylvania
In the Lake of the Woods
The Mind Game
Possession
Second Sight
24/7
A Winter Haunting

General Fiction

Coyote Cowgirl
The Ha-Ha
The Handmaid's Tale

The Inn at Lake Devine
The Memory Keeper's Daughter
The Memory of Running
Montana, 1948
The Time Traveler's Wife

Historical Fiction

Ahab's Wife, or, The Star-Gazer
Balzac and the Little Chinese Seamstress
The Blackbirder
The Captain's Wife
Cry, the Beloved Country
A Dangerous Road
The Dark Queen
Deafening
Doomsday Book
The Final Confession of Mabel Stark
Grand Ambition
Hearts and Bones
Hotel Transylvania
The Illuminator
The Iron Rose
The Keeper's Son
The Magnificent Savages
Memoirs of a Geisha
Moloka'i
Montana, 1948
Pompeii
The Red Tent
The Serpent in the Garden
The Spy's Kiss
Star of the Sea
These Is My Words
The Voyage of the Narwhal
Wake of the Perdido Star

Humorous Fiction

An Almost Perfect Moment
Coyote Cowgirl
The Dewey Decimal System of Love
Eat Cake

Good Grief
Good in Bed
The Good, the Bad, and the Ugly Men I've Dated
Her
Isn't It Romantic?
Match Me If You Can
Plain Heathen Mischief
Practical Demonkeeping: A Comedy of Horrors
The Rich Part of Life
Sister Betty! God's Calling You, Again!
The Trouble with Valentine's Day

Multicultural Fiction

An Almost Perfect Moment
Balzac and the Little Chinese Seamstress
Blood Ties
Cry, the Beloved Country
A Dangerous Road
The Kite Runner
The Inn at Lake Devine
Kite Runner
Life of Pi
Memoirs of a Geisha
Moloka'i
My Year of Meats
Sister Betty! God's Calling You, Again!
Sister of My Heart

Mystery

Bait
Blood Ties
A Dangerous Road
Death al Dente
The Defense
The Dewey Decimal System of Love
Five Mile House
Hearts and Bones
In the Lake of the Woods
Second Sight
The Serpent in the Garden
Trace Evidence

Nonfiction

Fat Girl: A True Story
Honor Lost: Love and Death in Modern-Day Jordan
In the Heart of the Sea: The Tragedy of the Whaleship Essex
Inside the Kingdom: My Life in Saudi Arabia
A Million Little Pieces
A Round-Heeled Woman: My Late-Life Adventures in Sex and Romance
Sunk without a Sound: The Tragic Colorado River Honeymoon of Glen and Bessie Hyde
Tender at the Bone: Growing Up at the Table

Romance

Archangel
The Dark Queen
The Dewey Decimal System of Love
The Good, the Bad, and the Ugly Men I've Dated
Her
Hotel Transylvania
The Illuminator
The Iron Rose
Match Me If You Can
The Mercy of Thin Air
Something Borrowed
The Spy's Kiss
The Time Traveler's Wife
The Trouble with Valentine's Day

Science Fiction

Archangel
Beggars in Spain
Childhood's End
Doomsday Book
The Eyre Affair
In the Garden of Iden
The Man Who Fell to Earth
The Terrorists of Irustan

Sea Adventures

The Blackbirder
The Captain's Wife

The Iron Rose
Life of Pi
The Magnificent Savages
Star of the Sea
The Voyage of the Narwhal
Wake of the Perdido Star

Women's Fiction

Ahab's Wife, or, The Star-Gazer
Angry Housewives Eating Bon Bons
Coyote Cowgirl
The Dewey Decimal System of Love
Eat Cake
Gods in Alabama
Good Grief
Good in Bed
The Handmaid's Tale
Hearts and Bones
Memoirs of a Geisha
My Sister's Keeper
My Year of Meats
The Red Tent
Sight Hound
Sister of My Heart
The Terrorists of Irustan
These Is My Words
Trace Evidence
The Yokota Officers Club

Selected Bibliography

Bodart, Joni. "Booktalks Do Work! The Effects of Booktalking on Attitude and Circulation." *Illinois Libraries* 68, no. 6 (June 1986): 378–81.
———. "The Effect of a Booktalk Presentation of Selected Titles on the Attitude toward Reading of Senior High School Students and on the Circulation of These Titles in the High School Library." PhD diss., Texas Women's University, 1985.
Crowther, Eleanor. "Booktalks/Read Alouds, Special Programs, and Service Projects to Encourage Middle School Student Participation in the Library." PhD diss., Nova University, 1993. ERIC# ED362850.
Grant-Williams, Renee. *Voice Power: Using Your Voice to Captivate, Persuade, and Command Attention.* New York: American Management Association, 2002.
Leeds, Dorothy. *PowerSpeak: the Complete Guide to Persuasive Public Speaking and Presenting.* New York: Prentice Hall, 1988.
Level, June Saine. "Booktalk Power—A Locally Based Research Study." *School Library Media Quarterly* 16 (Winter 1982): 154–55.
National Endowment for the Arts. *Reading at Risk: A Survey of Literary Reading in America.* Research Division Report #46. Washington, DC: Author, 2004, at www-.nea.gov/pub/ReadingAtRisk.pdf (accessed July 16, 2005).
Perlman, Alan M. *Writing Great Speeches: Professional Techniques You Can Use.* Boston: Allyn and Bacon, 1998.
Saricks, Joyce G., and Nancy Brown. *Reader's Advisory Service in the Public Library.* Chicago: American Library Association, 1997.
Theibert, Philip R. *How to Give a Damn Good Speech.* New York: Galahad, 2000.

Further Reading

Booher, Dianna. *Speak with Confidence: Powerful Presentations that Inform, Inspire and Persuade.* New York: McGraw-Hill, 2002.
  Learn the basics to get started and advanced techniques to fine-tune your delivery in order to maximize the impact on your audience.
Chelton, Mary K. "Booktalking: You Can Do It." *School Library Journal* 22, no. 8 (April 1976): 39–42.
  This basic instructional piece on booktalking techniques and benefits is geared toward young-adult librarians, but the advice is sound for adult booktalking as well.
Detz, Joan. *It's Not What You Say, It's How You Say It.* New York: St. Martin's Griffin, 2000.
  A renowned speech coach presents strategies and tips to organize and prepare speeches that will engage audiences.
Langemack, Chapple. *The Booktalker's Bible: How to Talk about the Books You Love to Any Audience.* Westport, CT: Libraries Unlimited, 2003.
  This helpful guide offers advice for all booktalkers, from the beginner to the more experienced, and it covers a wide variety of ages and settings.
Lawson, Karen. *Involving Your Audience.* Boston: Allyn and Bacon, 1999.
  This book contains many creative ideas for public speaking, including the use of props, humor, technology, storytelling, and audience participation techniques.
O'Keefe, Claudia. "Publicity 101: How to Promote Your Library's Next Event." *American Libraries* 36, no. 6 (June/July 2005): 52–55.
  This practical article offers six steps to launch a basic, no-frills media campaign, including instructions on how to write a press release.
Stuttard, Marie. *The Power of Speech: Effective Techniques for Dynamic Communication.* Hauppauge, NY: Barron's, 1997.
  The author's extensive experience in broadcasting, teaching, and performing enables her to offer helpful hints in delivering all types of speeches, whether for a beginner or an experienced speaker.
Wilder, Lilyan. *Seven Steps to Fearless Speaking.* New York: Wiley, 1999.

Get practical help to conquer many common public-speaking fears.
Wolfe, Lisa K. *Library Public Relations, Promotions, and Communications: A How-to-Do-It Manual*. New York: Neal-Schuman, 2005.
   This step-by-step manual offers valuable advice on planning and implementing a library PR program, including dozens of sample event plans, newsletters, brochures, press releases, and more.

Index

About the Authors

Ann-Marie Cyr lives in Mesa, Arizona, where she has been a librarian in the City of Mesa Library since 1989. She is a frequent presenter on booktalking topics at library association conferences and has given numerous booktalking presentations to the Mesa elementary schools.

Kellie Gillespie lives in Chandler, Arizona, with her husband and son. She has booktalked fiction titles with children, teens, and adults in a variety of settings and now serves as a fiction specialist at the City of Mesa Library. She regularly reviews new fiction, has published several articles, and is the author of *Teen Volunteer Services in Libraries* (2004).

R 028 Cy
, 2006

1491824

CPSIA information can be obtained
at www.ICGtesting.com
Printed in the USA
FSOW01n2232061117
40859FS

9 780810 854369